The Apache Gift
An Incredible Experience

Dale Flew...

Ed Sow...

The Apache Gift
An Incredible Experience

Dale Flowers
Ed Sowash

McCaa Books • Santa Rosa

McCaa Books

McCaa Books
1604 Deer Run
Santa Rosa, CA 95405

ISBN 978-1-7358074-5-4

First published in 2020 by McCaa Books,
an imprint of McCaa Publications.

Printed in the United States of America
Set in Minion Pro

Cover and book layout by Waights Taylor Jr.
Cover painting by Karen de la Peña
Dick Bass ink drawing by Dave Beronio

www.mccaabooks.com

Dedication

"To everyone who shared this time together at Vallejo High School."

Contents

FORWARD

THE AUTHORS WOULD LIKE to thank the class-mates and teammates who contributed to this story. We conducted 49 interviews that were both informative and often very enlightening. These interviews enriched the story and brought to light important facts and events that we had either forgotten or had no idea existed or occurred. More importantly, two fledgling writers discovered that our friends wanted this story to be told as much as we did. Besides the information gathered, the interviews were a source of motivation and inspiration for us to complete the undertaking.

What we have endeavored to do is capture the adventures we shared during the 1954 Vallejo High football season. It was a powerful experience that was seared into our minds and hearts.

For the record, Ed and I (Dale Flowers) are in our eighties, 83 and 84 to be exact. The contributors range in age from 81 to 86 years with Dorothy Bass the only exception. We know that there will be different versions and interpretations of our experiences we discovered during our interviews. In fact, the differences were ongoing as we prepared the book. We talked to several of our contributors more than once about a specific game or situation. Each time we talked, the particulars became clearer and a little more exacting. We get it. So, if you remember something differently than how it was portrayed and you really care, drop us a note and we will make the correction in the 2nd edition.

We hope you enjoy reading our story as much as we did writing it.

INTRODUCTION

TEN YEARS AGO, I (Ed Sowash) had this idea to write this book, or really have it written about the 1954 Apache Football Team—our team that was mentioned in *Sports Illustrated* as maybe the best team in the nation that year.

The article was about Dick Bass and they called him the best running back in the country, and the team, maybe the best in the country. I wanted the book to be about the '53 Team also, because they set the stage for the '54 Season.

I wanted the book to cover the key players in their developmental years in the Junior High programs in 1951 and 1952 and then into the '53 and '54 seasons of Vallejo High School. The three Junior Highs at that time were Vallejo, Franklin and recently opened Hogan.

I did research at the public library in town of all the articles from the *Vallejo Times Herald* Sports pages on microfiche and gave them to Jerry Strong, a coaching friend, who had written two books and he went to work.

He conducted interviews with players and started to write the book, but during the process he went legally blind and could not continue. He sent the research pages back to me and it sat in my files for several years.

Then I met Jim Hunt while working on the Vallejo Sports Hall of Fame Committee and he had written all the biographies of the inductees for 15 years, so I asked him to write the book and he agreed. I then sent all of the material to him in Utah and he started to go to work.

Long story short, he fell at home and died. Both were good men and good writers, but now the book looked like it would never be written.

A year passed and I was talking with my dear friend and teammate Dale Flowers, and the subject came up, and I said, "Dale, you should write the book." He is a very good writer and has authored Odes and Poems and dedicated them to several of our fallen teammates. At first he said, "No, too risky." Then he laughed and said, "Let's do it together." I quickly agreed. Two old friends started working together on a story that is dear to us both.

Here we go.

1

VALLEJO 1951–1954

VALLEJO WAS A BLUE-COLLAR working class city with Mare Island as the driver of the economy. Most of our parents worked at Mare Island or in one of the war related industries in the vicinity.

Our families came from all across the United States to Vallejo to fill the jobs needed in the war effort. Jerry Annoni described our community this way, "we were an amalgamation of people from all parts of the United States." For most of us, this was the first time we had experienced American diversity. Meeting and getting to know people who were different, with their own views and perspectives about the world was a new and challenging experience. Linda Nicol recalled vividly "coming from tiny Sonoma to Vallejo, I was struck by the wonder of it all, so many different people."

It was the same for others who came from Mississippi, North Dakota, New Mexico or other parts of the country. The first sight of a silver cloud of "blimps" or barrage balloons hovering over Vallejo was iconic and we understood we were in a different place at an unusual time.

The majority of our friends and classmates lived in one of the public housing projects spread around Vallejo: Chabot Terrace, Floyd Terrace, Carquinez Heights, Bay Terrace, Roosevelt Terrace and Federal Terrace. These micro communities were built primarily to house shipyard workers and military families engaged in World War II and later the Korea war effort.

Each housing project had schools, limited shopping, modern recreation centers, abundant open space, and public transportation. These Terraces were our neighborhoods and we identified with them with pride. "I'm from Chabot," or "I live in Floyd Terrace" was part of any introduction. We had a sense of community. One contributor suggested that the Terraces in many ways became the extended families that were left behind.

One feature of the Terraces is central to this story, the "The Rec Hall." This building was alive with activity, a gym, crafts, activities and the full array of sports programs. We spent hours at the Rec Hall, we met up with friends, competed in sports and kept out of trouble--as much as possible.

Our parents, teachers and coaches had lived through the Great Depression and World War II, the great social levelers of their time. These experiences shaped their perspectives on life. They understood what it meant to sacrifice for the common good and that value rubbed off on us. The majority of the families had only one bread winner. Our mothers were homemakers and there was plenty of neighborhood activity during the day. It seemed as though we were always being watched and could be tracked down when necessary. It was not uncommon to hear one mother call to another, " have you seen my rascal," and hear the reply " yes, he is here."

This environment instilled in us a sense of equality. After all, we lived in similar housing, attended similar schools, recreated in similar buildings and were cared for by the same health plan. Some differences and distinctions were there but they were more individualistic and less dramatic.

Vallejo downtown was the center of our social activity. There were five theaters, the Hanlon being the most prominent, to keep us entertained. The City of Paris, Crowleys, Penny's, Sears and Levee's department stores kept us well dressed. The China Barn, Plutos, Redtop Dairy, Fosters, Scotty's, Terry's and others kept us well nourished. Dragging Georgia Street and Tennessee Street and drives in-between kept us "cool" and in contact. And of course, the sports events, dances and parties on the weekend were what we did. We were socializers of the first order.

2

THE FARM SYSTEM

THE YEAR WAS 1951, Harry S Truman was our President, the Korean War was still going on, Congress passed the 22nd Amendment limiting the President to 2 terms, super glue was invented as well as Power Steering. The price of a new home was around $9,000 and the average Income was $ 2,799 a year. The cost of gas was 27 cents a gallon. Popular T.V. shows were *Gunsmoke, Bonanza, The Andy Griffith Show* and *Car 51 Where Are You?* Movies that year were *A Street Car Named Desire, The African Queen* and *Show Boat.*

The Vallejo Schools operated under the 6-4-4 system so your freshman and sophomore years were spent in junior high school and the junior and senior years were in high school which was combined with Vallejo Junior College. The junior college students and faculty gave the high school a relaxed atmosphere not found on most high school campuses. Three Junior High Schools, the Vallejo Junior High Papooses, the Franklin Junior High Braves, and The Hogan Junior High Warriors, all fielded football teams which were essentially the "The Farm System" for the Vallejo High School Apaches.

All the players we interviewed agreed that the experience and development attained in playing on the junior high teams was instrumental in the success we achieved as Apaches. We were well trained and prepared for high school football.

At our respective schools, we were the stars, the best football players that the school put on the field. We were at the top of the heap, however small. We played regular high school junior varsity teams which were usually made up of freshmen and sophomores with one important provision: in most programs, if you were good and the varsity needed your talent, you were promptly promoted to the varsity which was the main stage in high school football. In the Vallejo system, we freshmen and sophomores were stage central and the main attraction. No one swept up our talent for the benefit of the varsity. We played together for two seasons. This was a perfect situation for us to develop our talents, get special attention and build confidence in ourselves and our teammates.

We were taught the fundamentals, more accurately; the fundamentals were drilled into us until they became part of who we were. We learned how to block, tackle, kick, pass, run and beat our opponent. Our coaches were adamant about us understanding the fundamentals. They understood the connection between football fundamentals and success for our teams and for us as players in the future.

Steve McLemore recalled how this training in fundamentals helped make him a good football player. At Vallejo Junior High school, Steve played behind Owen Renz, the starting guard. On one occasion, Renz was thrown out of the game for hitting an opposing player over the head with his helmet, definitely not a fundamental taught or appreciated. Our helmets were leather and had no face guards; so it was like being slapped with a 16 ounce boxer's glove. No harm done. To Steve's utter surprise he heard Coach Biama yell, "Steve get in there." He did and not without considerable anxiety. "What do I do," Steve thought. He decided to do just what he had been taught in practice: block and tackle. This was Steve's first experience in playing competitive football and it proved successful. He learned he liked to hit people and he loved football. Steve had learned the fundamentals and he was rewarded.

We learned how to win. After all, the purpose of a game is to win. All the Junior High teams experienced winning seasons during this time period. Players from Hogan did not lose a game for the two seasons and winning was all they knew. Both Vallejo and Franklin had winning seasons, Vallejo was 6-2 in 1951 and Franklin was 5-3 in 1952. In the two seasons, the three teams won 38 games and lost 10. There is something intangible but very real about winning. It feels good, it is uplifting and winning feeds on itself. You want to keep winning. Conversely, losing is a real drag. It is not an exaggeration to say our players and coaches and parents expected to win every game. High expectations are powerful motivators and we had them.

We were tough. It was part of the ethos of Vallejo football. At Hogan, Coach Mal Simpson was sometimes over the edge. Our practices were very close to torture and could never happen today. We had two practices a day for the first week. Mrs. Simpson would make peanut butter and jelly sandwiches for lunch. On one occasion, ants invaded the lunch. The sandwiches were served and we ate them. We blew and brushed the ants off as best we could but Ed Sowash recalls, "I ate my sandwich, ants and all, with no complaint." Coach Simpson loved Ed's devotion to the game. Hogan practiced on a hard dirt field, no grass. Franklin's field sounded more dreadful. Before their first practice, they had a tractor come in and plow the field and then the players stomped around breaking up the clods before practice. Biama stressed hard hitting and hurting your opponents and Vallejo had the two toughest kids we ever knew, Pete Kalamaras and Bill Wilson. The net result was that the Apaches were going to possess toughness. We were never intimidated by another team. We were tough and good and we knew it.

Best of all, we got to play a lot and gain invaluable experience. You had the opportunity to find out if football was truly your game.

Think about it, it was like having three junior varsity teams funneling into one high school. In our particular case, there was even more; there was exceptional talent.

During the two seasons, you can see the emergence of the starters and key players who would become 1954 Apaches. Hogan sent Dick and Norman Bass, DL Hurd, Ed Sowash and Dale Flowers. Vallejo offered Pete Kalamaras, Tom Zunino, Bill Wilson and Bernie Fleming. Franklin delivered Ron Stover, Don Fell, Dave Edington and Bob Coronado. This was the package The Farm System produced in 1952. It was an array of talented players who would make up the 1954 Apaches. There was no doubt Coach Bob Patterson and coach Dave Thomas would be delighted with this crop.

3

JUNIOR HIGH COACHES

OUR JUNIOR HIGH COACHES were close to the best. They were dedicated teachers who taught us how to play football. They possessed very different temperaments and approaches to the game. When we met them they were early in their careers, Coach Simpson had been coaching 4 years, Coach Coke Morrison only 2 years and Coach Dick Biama was a rookie. They were young and relatively inexperienced as coaches but as men they were quite special. They had all volunteered and served honorably in the United States Military in World War II. They had lived through the Great Depression.

Coach Mal Simpson taught physical education at Vallejo Junior High and instituted a very successful intramural program. He was asked to coach the football team. He resisted at first, saying that he had not played the game and did not know much about football. Nonetheless, he accepted and was encouraged to get a book and learn the game. Bob Rodrigo, who played on Simpson's first team, recalled Simpson's first talk. He brought out the book on football fundamentals and explained to his players that he had never played or coached football before and they would learn the game together. He promised them only one thing, they would be the best conditioned team on the field.

Throughout his tenure as a coach, he was true to his word, his teams were always that. He emphasized the fundamentals of blocking, tackling and doing your job. One of his teaching techniques was to run the same play over and over until it was a touchdown. His strategy for winning games was quite simple: wear the opponent down and win the game. He started slow, 2 wins in his first year, 2 loses in his second year, and then proceeded to 5 undefeated seasons and in his last year of coaching, he lost only one game, that was to Franklin.

Coach Simpson was a strict disciplinarian, but fair with his players. There were no favorites and no exceptions for any behaviors that violated his norms. Don Rodrigo, describes an incident where he made inappropriate comments to a staff person in the cafeteria before coming to practice. Someone reported the incident to Simpson. Don, who was the starting quarterback, was held out of the next game without explanation. With minutes remaining, Coach Simpson called Don over and let him know that his behavior toward the staff person was unacceptable and could not happen again. Don agreed and coach sent him into the game.

As one teammate described Coach Simpson: "Mal built character in you whether you liked it or not." Every player gained from the time spent with Coach Simpson. Doug Stone explained that he was the father figure and mentor he needed at that time in his life. Doug was not alone.

Like Mal Simpson, "Coke" Morrison had not played football: he was a basketball coach. He too learned football from a book.

We imagine that he went to Mal Simpson and asked "how do I coach football?" Simpson went to his bookshelf, took down his football bible and gave it to Morrison with the simple explanation: "It works". It is worth mentioning that all these coaches were good friends and competitors. "Coke" was most proud of the one and only victory over Hogan in Simpson's last year.

"Coke" was a bit of an innovator. He tried different systems and arranged weekly scrimmages with St. Vincent's High School every week. The players loved it: no practice and they would get to play a game. This gave his players some valuable experience while having a little fun. Bob Coronado and Don Fell described "Coke" as even tempered and easy going, never screamed or ranted. His was a good communicator, easy to understand, respected and well-liked by the players. He loved to dance and in our crowd that made him pretty cool.

Of all the coaches, Dick Biama had the most football experience. He stared as the quarterback on the 1947 Vallejo Junior College team that played for the State Championship. He transferred to Fresno State and was the starting quarterback for two years.

He became the Head football coach at Vallejo Junior High in 1950. Biama knew the game, he knew strategy and he was a great teacher.

Tom Zunino thought Coach Biama was the best quarterback coach he knew in his career. Biama was stern, but fair. He saw what talent you had and helped you exploit it.

Bernie Fleming recalled, when Coach Biama saw how your ability would work at the next level, he made a recommendation with enthusiasm. Bernie thought Biama's recommendation to Patterson was in part why he was a starter as a junior on the Apaches.

Coach Biama thought about his players futures as football players and students. He was a source of inspiration and motivation for his players.

We can fairly conclude, these men were dedicated teachers and coaches who cared about us as individuals and as football players. They were great role models. One of our teammates, who taught and coached high school for twenty years, observed that the 1954 Apaches were a very coachable group of athletes. These three coaches contributed significantly to that truth.

We had been around great coaches for years in the Vallejo Recreation District program and in

Vallejo schools at all levels in all sports. The majority of our teammates excelled in one or more sports. There was a lot of interaction between players and many different coaches. We valued coaching and fortunately for us , we were favored with a group of savvy and committed coaches. Another telltale sign of why these coaches were so effective was that many of our teammates went into coaching and teaching for their life's work.

These coaches would guide our football lives for the next two years.

4

THE 1951 JUNIOR HIGH SEASON

IN OUR INTERVIEWS, we asked, "Why were we such a great team?" Almost everyone agreed we were a close knit group. We were a team and we played as a team and we won as a team. We developed teamwork skills and attitudes in The Farm System under the tutelage of our coaches. It was a tacit expectation to be a team player. The team development of the '54 Apaches began in 1951 and matured in the '54 season. This was a time when we would be playing with and against each other for two years. We got to know and respect each other as football players and friends.

We are going to go through all the games briefly to give you some sense of what it was like. A friend who looked over our manuscript remarked, "It's a lot like going through a washing machine's cycles, you must go through each one to get a clean product.

WEEK ONE

Papooses Win

The Papooses routed Armijo Junior Varsity 41-0. Six different players scored touchdowns: Jim Ledoux, Johnny Eaton, Mark Cameron, Leon Wilson in the first half, and Jack Carmichael and George Hawkins in the second half. The coach praised his team for keeping intact their 25 wins in a row. Biama gave special praise to Owen Renz, Jim Salisbury and Mark Cameron for their down field blocking.

Hogan Wins

Hogan opened its first football season with a 40-6 win over Crockett. This was Dick Bass's debut and he did not disappoint. "Ramblin" Richard, as he came to be known, ran for three touchdown and made runs setting up a fourth. He was a ninth grader, 5' 8" and 145 pounds, but he was fast and elusive. Nate Peterson ran for a score and Don Rodrigo led the Warriors on a 60 yard drive finishing with a 15 yard pass to Billy Glover for the touchdown. Everyone on the team had a chance to play.

Times-Herald Sports Editor Dave Beronio's comment: "Dick Bass was something special."

Franklin Loses

Taking advantage of three Franklin fumbles, Stockton defeated Franklin 21-6 at Corbus Field. In the second quarter, Franklin fumbled on their own 9 yard line. Stockton scored on the next play and led 6-0. In the 2nd quarter, Franklin scored on an end around by Baldwin Ellis who ran 36 yards for the score. The score tied 6-6 but Franklin would not score again. Stockton scored twice and forced a safety in the 4th quarter.

Standouts for the Braves were Dick Tharp and Ron Stover.

WEEK TWO

Hogan Wins

Hogan ended the Papooses 25 game win streak. The Warriors defeated the Vallejo Papooses 25-7 in a game played at Corbus Field. The Papooses scored first, when Ozzie Hines intercepted a Don Rodrigo pass deep in the Warriors territory for a score. Hogan came back to score 4 touchdowns and end the Papooses 25 game win string. Coach Simpson highlighted the strong play of Dick Bass, Don Rodrigo and Nate Peterson and praised the the play of the entire team for staying focused after the early turnover. He announce that they would get their game uniforms for the rest of the season. For some reason, in both seasons, the Warriors did not get their game uniforms until the second or third game.

Franklin Wins

Franklin Braves outplayed Crockett in a 33-6 romp. Coach Morrison directed his team to their first win. Franklin was unstoppable. Bob Stafford accounted for three of the five touchdowns scored. Coach Morrison singled out the play of Stafford, Bennie Ellis, Ron Stover, Roger Maki and Baldwin Ellis.

WEEK THREE

Hogan Wins

Hogan walloped Franklin, 51-13. Don Gleason reported, "without a doubt one of the finest junior high football teams ever seen on a local gridiron." The Hogan Warriors, scored every time they had the ball. One memorable moment was when Billie Estes galloped 73 yards for a touchdown, but the play was called back, off sides. On the next play, Billie Glover ran 78 yards for a score that was called back, off sides again. On the very next play, Billie Estes runs 83 yards for the touchdown, no penalty this time. Breakaway runs, a fine passing and vicious downfield blocking marked the Hogan play throughout the game. Hogan had an array of fine running backs with speed and power.

Vallejo Wins

Papooses dumped Tamalpais Junior Varsity 37-0. With terrific downfield blocking, the Papooses scored five touchdowns on the ground and one through the air to defeat Tamalpais 37-0. Mark Cameron ran 30 yards for the first score. In the second period John Eaton finished a drive with a 15 yard dash to the end zone. In the third period Ozzie Hines blocked a punt and Hal Lundblad picked up the ball and ran 35 yards for the touchdown. Tom Zunino connected on a flat pass to Bernie Fleming for a score. George Hawkins scored the clincher when he ran 65 yards to pay dirt.

WEEK FOUR

Hogan Wins

Dick Bass put on a one-man show as the Hogan Warriors defeated the Benicia Junior Varsity 39-13. Bass scored in every quarter on runs of 45, 60, 65 and a pass reception from Don Rodrigo for 35 yards and a touchdown. Albert Jones ran 40 yards for his first touchdown and LaVerne Pratt picked up a fumble and galloped into the end zone dragging three defenders hanging on to him. Coach Simpson cleared the bench in the second half.

Franklin Wins

The Franklin Braves defeated the Petaluma Junior Varsity 29-12. Bob Stafford scored three of the Braves touchdowns and Gail Haworth made the fourth. The Franklyn defense played well, led by Ron Stover and Ray Kenny.

Papooses Win

Vallejo Junior High recorded their third victory in four outings with a 47-8 romp over the Drake Junior Varsity. Jack Carmichael provided the highlight of the day was a 98 yard touchdown run. John Eaton ran for two touchdowns, one for 55 yards, the other for 35. Every back on the team scored. Great line and downfield blocking made it seem easy. A hard charging defensive line led by Fred Gardner, Harold Lundblad and Owen Renz contained Drake.

WEEK FIVE

Papooses Win

Times-Herald writer John Larson wrote "Napa Junior High School's vaunted football team, tabbed as good enough to represent most small four-year high schools, is back in Napa this morning somewhat bewildered by the 34-24 trouncing handed them yesterday afternoon by the Vallejo Junior High Papooses. The Papooses, throwing the rough stuff back at the Knight's face just as fast as the visitors put it out, out-blocked, out-tackled and out ran the Blue and Gold at every turn. Although the issue was in doubt throughout the first three quarters, the Papooses were never behind after they jumped off to a 7-0 lead early in the first quarter. George Hawkins accounted for the first Vallejo touchdown. Leon Wilson scored next with a 31 yard touchdown sprint behind superb blocking. Papooses marked up three TDs in the third quarter. It was a great day for the Green and the White, winning their forth game of the season.

Hogan Wins

The undefeated Warriors rolled to their fifth victory with a 40-12 win over the Tamalpais Junior Varsity. Hogan ran for five touchdowns: Billie Glover raced 30 yards, Richard Bass circled end for 49 yards; Nathan Peterson picked up a fumble and ran 20 yards; Glover bolted through the middle for 30 yards; and Bass around end for 20 yards. Bill Estes broke his leg in the game and will miss the balance of the season. Hogan was loaded with running backs.

Franklin Wins

Franklin Junior High scored four touchdowns in the first half and coasted to a 33-12 victory over the Drake Junior Varsity. Drake did not make a first down until the third quarter. Franklin scoring: Dick Tharp plunged over from the 3. Charlie Bansuelo went 10 yards around end. Bansuelo passed 40 yards to Willie Santiago. Santiago galloped 50 yards through the center, and Santiago scored again from 58 yards out. Franklin's defense was stifling.

WEEK SIX

Hogan Wins

Undefeated Hogan recorded its sixth victory in easy fashion with a 40-13 romp over the Drake Junior Varsity. Nathan Peterson scored two Hogan touchdowns on a 30 yard run and the other on an intercepted pass for a touchdown. Dick Bass scored twice, one a 75 yard broken field run to remember, behind blocking all the way down the field. DL Hurd emerged from the shadows and recorded two touchdowns, one a 45 yard pounding run for a touchdown.

Franklin Loses

Franklin traveled to Napa and dropped a 12-6 decision to Napa Junior High. Franklin's lone touchdown, came in the fourth quarter when Bob Stafford ran 55 yards to score. Napa scored in the first quarter with a drive of 60 yards, and recorded the winning touchdown in the final minute of the first half on a 65 yard punt return.

Papooses Lose

Vallejo lost to Petaluma Junior Varsity 20-0 in a "fluky" game. The game was scoreless until late in the third quarter. A Papoose fumble on their own three yard line and a quick score by Petaluma was unsettling. Petaluma scored two more touchdowns in the fourth quarter.

WEEK SEVEN

Franklin Wins

Scoring in each of the first three quarters, the Franklin Braves defeated the Tamalpais Junior Varsity 27-6. Bob Stafford started the offense with a 17 yard dash to pay dirt. Jerry Howell corralled the Tamalpais quarterback behind the goal line for a safety and 2 points. Bill Webb passed 15 yards to Roger Maki for a touchdown, and then threw 23 yards to Willie Santiago for the score. In the final period, Franklin lineman Bennie Ellis recovered a Tamalpais fumble in the end zone.

Hogan Wins

Dick Bass romped to four touchdowns and paced Hogan to a 34-14 victory over a very good Petaluma Junior Varsity team. In leading Hogan to its seventh win, Bass raced for touchdowns on runs of 9, 40,

70, and 95 yards. Nathan Peterson scored the other Hogan touchdown on a 10 yard dive play.

The 95 yard run by Bass was a prelude to the future. One of those runs that never seem to end, first they have him, then they don't have him, then he is in the end zone. We will get to see many more in the next four years.

Vallejo Wins

Crockett forfeits to Vallejo.

WEEK EIGHT

Vallejo Wins

Exploding for two touchdowns in the final four minutes of play, the Papooses rolled to a 32-19 victory over the Franklin in the ninth renewal of their annual grid classic. Johnny Eaton scored four touchdowns, including an 81 yard kickoff return and an 89 yard run that fell one yard short of a touchdown. The score was 13-12 at half time and stayed competitive until the Papooses broke it open in the fourth quarter. Bill Wilson blocked a Franklin punt and Eaton scored four plays later. Vallejo now led 19 to 13. Their next drive started on the Franklin 3 and in five plays Eaton scored again. Jim Ledoux set up the final score when he intercepted a Bob Stafford pass on the 30 yd. line and returned it to Franklin's 45 yd. line. Three plays later, Leon Wilson put the game away, scoring from the 12 yard line. This was a hard fought game from beginning to end.

Hogan Wins.

Hogan completed an undefeated season with a 6-0 hard fought victory over Napa. The lone score of the thriller came with four minutes of play remaining when Don Rodrigo handed off to Billy Glover, who rammed through the middle from seven yards out for the touchdown. The Hogan defense won the game. Napa's only threat came in the second quarter when they marched to the Hogan five yard line and were stranded. Glover, Rodrigo and Nate Peterson sparked the defense to assure an undefeated season.

1951 SEASON CONCLUSION

The 1951 season ended with The Farm System producing three good football teams, Hogan was the top team but Vallejo and Franklin were competitive. We were getting what it meant to use the "we" as Dick Bass would often say, "there ain't no 'I' in "team," and his commitment to the team concept was consequential. Most importantly, a talented cohort of football players were getting to know and respect one another.

5

THE 1952 SEASON

THE 1952 SEASON WAS DIFFERENT. These three junior high teams will make up the 1954 Apaches.

In a very real sense we are now playing with and against each other in an unusual ongoing practice. We think that at on some level, we all knew we would eventually be on the same team. Our games with each other were competitive, hard fought and often spirited.

Coach Simpson gave a talk before the Hogan-Vallejo game that his players remember to this day. He told his players in so many words they were the "real Americans and those guys on the hill were not. Now go out there and show them how to play football." The Warriors literally ran over each other to get at the Papooses. Franklin only beat Hogan one time in Coach "Coke" Morrison's tenure as coach.

"Coke" referred often to his win over Hogan and Coach Simpson as one of the highlights of his coaching career. It was the only defeat for Hogan in six years. Beating Hogan was special and his players picked up on it. The Franklin games were always contested vigorously. In any case, our coaches knew where we were headed and understood that we were all on the same team. There was extraordinary talent in this cohort of players and Bob Patterson understood this better than anyone.

This was the season when the 1954 Apaches came alive and we started getting to know each other as players and friends.

WEEK ONE

Papooses Win

The Vallejo Junior High School Papooses out toughed the Edison Vikings 24-14 victory. The Papooses marshaled a three-touchdown rally in the second half that carried them to a victory. Tom Zunino led the attack with two touchdown passes and fine running to secure the last touchdown.

Hogan Wins

Dick Bass performed an amazing one man scoring show leading Hogan to a 45-19 win over Stockton. Bass scored six touchdowns, on runs of 60, 45, 72 and 98 yards. His other two scores came on a punt return for 60 yards and a kickoff return for 95 yards. He was seemingly unstoppable and Hogan was on track.

Franklin Wins

Franklin scored five touchdowns in the first half and an extra one for good measure in the fourth quarter to give the Braves a 39-6 opening game victory over the Tamalpais Junior varsity. Bob Coronado scored twice and intercepted a pass stopping a Tamalpais drive. Don Fell and Dave Edington were standouts on defense. Three wins for Vallejo teams. Dick Bass, Tom Zunino and Bob Coronado were immediate standouts.

WEEK TWO

Papooses Win

After a scoreless first half, the Papooses scored four touchdowns in the last two periods to defeat Stockton Junior High 25-13 in a hard fought game. Gale Bean led the Papooses scoring three short yardage touchdowns. Leon Wilson registered the fourth TD on a 65 yard gallop with Tackle Bill Wilson opening a hole and clearing the way. Coach Biama praised his entire team for the victory and singled out guard Steve McLemore for providing the spark that ignited the attack in the second half. However Steve could not remember what it was he did that ignited his team.

Hogan Wins

Hogan defeated Franklin 13-0 for the win. The game was scoreless for three and one half quarters. The Warriors scored twice in the final five minutes of the game to win going away. The spectacular play of the game was a double reverse with Norman Bass going in for the score. Three minutes later DL Hurd waltzed 22 yards for the second touchdown. Hogan is undefeated with 10 wins without a loss.

For three and one half quarters it was a see-saw melee with both teams playing hard nosed defense. Franklin's determined defensive play completely bottled up Dick Bass. This was first and only time Dick failed to score a touchdown in two seasons of play. He twisted his ankle in the first period and did not play the rest of the game. DL Hurd and Louis Davenport carried the load the rest of the game.

Coach Simpson's football strategy of wear your opponent down and win the game was in full display in the Franklin game.

WEEK THREE

Franklin Wins

Franklin scored a 20-6 over Napa before 300 fans. Franklin's Jim Price rambled 35 yards for touchdown and a 6-0 lead. Napa scored in the second quarter to tie the game at 6-6, at halftime. In the third quarter Mike Campas passed 20 yards to Otis Grimble for the second touchdown. Bill Stewart powered 15 yards for the third touchdown on a power play for Franklyn's final touchdown. Jim Price, Bob Coronado and Bill Stewart provided a solid ground attack. Otis Grimble and Don Fell led an outstanding defensive effort against a solid Napa team.

Hogan Wins

DL Hurd led Hogan to a 24-6 win over Edison. Hurd scored four touchdowns, on power runs of 10, 5, 6 and 5 yards. Although DL made the scores, it was the combined running of DL and Lou Davenport that carried the day. The Hogan defense held Edison to one score on a trick play in the forth quarter. Dick Bass did not play because of an injury.

Papooses Lose

Playing "ball control," Petaluma Junior Varsity defeated the Papooses 19-18. Both teams racked up three touchdowns early in the game and Petaluma made one extra point. Leon Wilson provided the thrill of the day with a 85 yard kickoff return for a touchdown. Pete Kalamaras and Bill Wilson were singled out for their fine play on offense and defense.

WEEK FOUR

Papooses Win

Roy Adams' passing propelled the Papooses to their third victory in four starts with a 27-0 win over the Drake Junior Varsity. Adams passed to Leon Wilson for 20 yards for Vallejo's first TD. Adams and Wilson teamed up again with a 65 yard touchdown play. Roy did not stop throwing and his third touchdown was a perfect strike to Gail Bean for 18 yards. Adams scored the fourth touchdown on a 3 yard quarter back sneak. Roy was the back-up to Tom Zunino who was injured.

Hogan Wins

Hogan throttles Tamalpais 26-6. Dick Bass scored three touchdowns on runs of 30, 45 and 10 yards. Don Robbins passed 20 yards to Norman Bass for the fourth score of the day. Hogan's defense throttled

Tamalpais and the Warriors are now undefeated in their last 12 games.

Franklin Loses

Stockton whipped Franklin 33-0 in a game played in Stockton. Fumbles, mistakes and missing key players was the story in this loss. The two fumbles resulted in two touchdowns early. It might have been the heat, or the delta water but, whatever the cause, it was downright ugly.

"It's not the first time that a junior high football team has fallen apart under fire, and it won't be the last. Teenage boys are apt to do anything when the going gets rough," the Vallejo Times Herald opined. The story was not funny and not appreciated.

WEEK FIVE

Franklin Wins

In a complete reversal from the previous week, Franklin soundly defeated the Drake Junior Varsity 33-0. Jim Himes passed for three Franklin touchdowns and two conversions to lead the Braves attack. Himes first touchdown throw was a 15 yard strike to Les Lundblad. Himes next scoring throw was a perfect 40 yard strike to Otis Grimble. Himes and Lundblad teamed up again with a 35 yard strike for the touchdown. Franklin could still muster a respectful ground game, and Jim Price scored on a 45 yard run over tackle. The Braves defense stopped the Drake team cold with Don Fell and

Mickey Jameyson the bulwarks in the Franklin defensive line.

Hogan Wins

Hogan ground out a 34-6 victory over Vallejo Jr. High at Corbus Field before 1,000 fans. Hogan's running game, led by Dick Bass, Jim Davenport and DL Hurd, was overpowering. The Warriors are 5-0. Ed Sowash's blocked punt set up one touchdown. In another outstanding play, Sowash unleashed a block on three defenders who had trapped Dick on the sideline. There were three and then there were none and Dick went the rest of the way untouched for the score. Dick's running was extraordinary and beautiful to see. His end sweeps seemed unstoppable and good for big yardage anytime. Team blocking is improving each game and Hogan's defense held strong all day.

WEEK SIX

Papooses Win

Touchdown drives in the first, third and fourth quarters spurred Vallejo to a 20-7 victory over the Tamalpais Junior Varsity. A 12 yard pass from Roy Adams to Bernie Fleming accounted for Vallejo's first score early in the first quarter. Gilman Thompson blasted 12 yards into the end zone for another. The Papooses added an insurance touchdown after recovering a Tamalpais fumble, driving 40 yards and Leon Wilson went the last 8 yards for the score. Fullback Thompson was the offensive player of the game. Standouts in the line were Bernie Fleming, Owen Renz and Bill Wilson.

Hogan Wins

Dick Bass ran for four touchdowns to lead Hogan Junior High to a 32-14 win over the Drake Junior Varsity. Bass started early on his touchdown jaunts. Bass returned a punt 60 yards for a touchdown. Bass passed to Willie Kelley for the conversion. Bass scored two more touchdowns runs, one for 60 yards, another for 28. Hogan's defense was stifling in holding Drake to two scores.

Franklin Loses

The Petaluma Junior Varsity found a weakness in the Franklin Junior High pass defense and threw for four touchdowns as they garnered a 25-19 victory. Franklin's Bill Stewart ran for two touchdowns and Bob Coronado added the third with a spectacular 90 yard kickoff return for the touchdown. Stewart, the fleet fullback broke loose around end and outran the Petaluma defense for 62 yards and the score. Three series of plays later Stewart went over again, this time on a 15 yard sprint, also around end. But Franklin could not contain Petaluma's passing game. The loss left Franklin with a 3-3 record to date.

WEEK SEVEN

Franklin Wins

Franklin defeated Stockton, 13-7 in a close, tough fought battle on the Stockton High School field.

Franklin scored first, as in the second quarter Bill Stewart bolted 55 yards off tackle for the first touchdown. Bob Coronado raced 25 yards around end for the second score. Stockton's only score came on a trick pass run play. Franklin's defense secured the victory. Ben Carmichael and Otis Grimble drew special praise for their all-around play.

Hogan Wins

Hogan overpowered Petaluma High School's junior varsity, 31-6. The Warriors took the kickoff and drove 70 yards for their first score with Lou Davenport legging it the last five. On Hogan's next series, Dick Bass broke loose for a 40 yard touchdown sprint. The Warriors scored twice in the second quarter. DL Hurd capped a 60 yard drive with a five yard blast into the end zone. Tackle Keith Bohanon set up the next touchdown by blocking and recovering a punt on the Petaluma 16 yard line. Bass took over from there and scored on the first play from scrimmage. Petaluma broke in with its only score early in the fourth quarter, with a six-yard pass, after a 55 yard drive. Dick Bass set up the final touchdown by firing a 30 yard pass to Norman Bass who carried the ball another 12 yards for the score. Tackle Ed Sowash booted the extra point. Hogan has fifteen straight wins.

Papooses lose

A safety in the third quarter, when a hard charging Napa line caught quarterback Roy Adams behind his own goal line for a touch back, gave the Napa Knights a 21-19 victory over the Vallejo Papooses. The Knights went ahead by two touchdowns early in the game on a pair of sustained drives, neither score was converted. Leon Wilson scored twice on a 35 yard dash for one and took a pass from Tom Zunino for the other. The conversions were not good. Gail Bean made the last score with a 84 yard touchdown run. Missed extra points were the story for this loss.

WEEK EIGHT

Franklin Wins

A five-year jinx was finally smashed when the Franklin Braves slammed Vallejo for a convincing 14-0 victory with 1,000 plus chilled fans watching. Franklin's first score came early in the second quarter on a beautiful piece of running by Bill Stewart on a 60 plus yard drive. The score remained 7 - 0 until the final minute when Stan Glass went the final four yards over guard for the score. Franklin's defense was superb throughout the game.

Ron Stover and Bob Coronado did not play together at Franklin. Bob's mother would not let him play as a 9th grader, and Ron was hurt in the 10th. We can only imagine how much better Franklin would have been with both players on the field.

Hogan Wins

Hogan defeats Napa 29-13 and are the North Bay League Champions. The Warriors have won 16 straight games and have completed two perfect seasons. Bass opened the Hogan scoring in the first quarter by romping 35 yards for a touchdown. In the second quarter, DL Hurd capped a 50 yard drive by going over from the seven. Bass followed with a 67 yard touchdown run. Don Robbins passed to Willie Kelley for a touchdown. Hurd sacked the Napa quarterback behind the goal line for a safety. In the third period, Nat Lessier recovered a fumble and Hurd punched it in for the touchdown. Napa scored twice in the fourth quarter, as Coach Simpson emptied the bench. Bass and Hurd were Hogan's version of the Army greats Glen Davis and Doc Blanchard, Mr Inside and Mr. Outside. Looking back now, we believe Dick & DL were the best, speed and power incarnate.

Conclusion of the 1952 Season

The season was over and these teams had pretty good records. The Vallejo teams won 32 games and lost 10. Hogan was undefeated. Vallejo and Franklin had winning seasons, Vallejo was 6- 2 in 1951 and Franklin was 5 - 3 in 1952. Richard Bass was introduced to the world, Dave Beronio would take Dick to football banquets around the Bay Area and introduce him, saying, "You watch this kid. He's gonna make it big."

1952 Junior High School All Star Offensive Team

1952 Junior High School All Star Defensive Team

6

THE FARM SYSTEM RESULTS

THE 1952 SEASON WAS OVER and the two years spent in The Farm System was complete. The Farm System delivered our cohort of solid football players. We had a better understanding of the game and we learned football fundamentals. We learned about ourselves and about the players from the other schools. Most importantly, we gained experience, self-confidence and motivation to play at the next level. The Farm System produced a cohort of football players that would comprise the 1954 Apaches.

The players selected to the 1952 Vallejo All City Teams were impressive. These players would become the starters and key players on the 1954 Apaches. The Farm System did its job. We were well prepared to compete at the next level. These were the athletes Coach Bob Patterson and Assistant Coach Dave Thomas would inherit.

Patterson and Thomas were part of The Farm System in a unique and important way, they officiated the Junior High football games. Willis McJunkin, a master official himself, related how officials are part of the game and, at the same time, watching the players closely. They get to know the players on a lot of levels. Patterson and Thomas were good officials and they knew us as players and how we might fit into Patterson's unique "short punt" system.

The coaches were a club. They were friends working together, coaching more than one sport, competing against each other and teaching in the same school system.

They shared information that was helpful to everyone involved. Bernie Fleming believed that Coach Biama made the recommendation that made Bernie the starting end as a junior.

The first time you met Coach Patterson he seemed to know you. For sure, he knew a lot about you as a football player. He would go to the Junior High Sports Rallies and invite athletes to come out for sports. He would tell stories, share a few expectations and answer questions. Patterson was a motivator and communicator with a wry sense of humor. Norman Bass tells the story when the 1955 Apaches were playing Riordan at Kezar Stadium in San Francisco and were losing at half time. They were not playing well, nothing was going right. At the half, the players were waiting for the coach to come in give them hell, time went by and no coach, no one is saying anything, then there is a loud pounding on the door, Patterson looked in and around and said, " Sorry ladies I must be in the wrong locker room," and left. Norman said, "We went out there and kicked the shit out of them."

We were off to a good start. We were well pre-pared to be Apaches, thanks to The Farm System.

The 1952 Vallejo All City Team

The All City Teams, offense and defense, would become the 1954 Vallejo High Champions. The offensive team included Dick Bass, DL Hurd, Tom Zunino, Ed Sowash, Bernie Fleming, Dave Edington, Don Fell and Ron Stover. The defensive team included DL Hurd, Bob Coronado, Don Fell, Leon Wilson, Dale Flowers, Pete Kalamaras, Bill Wilson and Bernie Fleming. These all-stars represented the Hogan, Franklin and Vallejo Jr. Highs. This was the group that would make up the 1954 Apaches. These were the athletes Coach Patterson and Thomas would inherit.

Coaches' Patterson and Thomas knew who these players were and how they might fit into the next two years as Apaches. These coaches, Simpson, Morrison, Biama, Patterson and Thomas talked and knew each other well. They all coached more than one sport, competed against each other, worked in the same school system and were part of the Vallejo football tradition. But Patterson and Thomas went one important step further; they were referees for the Junior High games. They had close up looks at all of us. They knew or had a good idea where or how we might fit into their system. Ed Sowash remembered that Patterson was officiating a game and saw him make a play where he knocked down three opposing players with one bone jarring block. He was an early starter when he got to the Apaches. Coach Patterson had another technique that was very helpful in bringing players into the fold, he would go to sport rallies at each Junior High and invite players to come out for football and other sports. He would share stories, share a few expectations and answer questions. He made you feel welcome and special.

We were prepared for the next step.

7

1953 VALLEJO APACHES FOOTBALL SEASON

IN THE WORDS OF MARK CAMERON, Co-Captain of the 1953 Apaches, "There can be little doubt that the 1953 football experience played an important role in the success of the 1954 'Dream Team.'" We agreed whole heartedly with Mark's judgment. At the end of the '53 season, we had gained valuable experience, self-confidence, a bit of humility and the emerging conviction that we could be really good.

This is what happened, before the season was over, the juniors would make significant contributions to the success of the 1953 Apaches. Dick scored 31 touchdowns, Ron Stover, Bernie Fleming, Pete Kalamaras, Ed Sowash and DL Hurd were key players in all our wins. To be clear, at that time, we were not thinking about the next season. We just wanted to play and win and be part of a great team. Looking back now 65 years later, it is quite clear to us that the 1953 Apache season was a second underpinning for the '54 Apaches and a perfect season.

Vallejo 39 Lodi 9

The Lodi game was the coming out party for Dick Bass and the San Francisco Bay Area football world. Dick scored five TD's in a 39 - 9 triumph over Lodi. It was an amazing performance and a preview of what was to come. Bass streaked to the end zone on runs of 31, 18, 52, 73, and 41 yards. Three of the scores came within a nine minute span in the third period. He was sprung loose by efficient, often bone jarring blocking. It was a close game until the third quarter when Bass and the Apaches busted the game wide open and take a solid lead of 28-7.

Vallejo put the first points of the season on the scoreboard seven minutes into the game. Don Rodrigo recovered a Lodi fumble and Bass scored on the next play. Rodrigo's conversion attempt was low and blocked. He made up for the miss by kicking a 32 yard field goal before the half. With five minutes remaining, Vallejo had the ball on its own 41, Bass in the deep spot, took the pass from center and one could sense the former Hogan Junior High star would once again go all the way. He rolled wide and sped down the sidelines to score for the fifth time. A crunching block by Johnnie Eaton cleared the lanes. The entire Vallejo team deserved praise. Bass had fine downfield blocking and our line cracked open holes and Dick did the rest.

The juniors were having an immediate impact; Ron Stover and Bernie Fleming were the starting ends; DL Hurd and Pete Kalamaras on defense and

Ed Sowash on offense were moving into starting roles. Another silver lining in the Lodi game, by racking up a big score, more reserves got playing time and game experience. This would be the pattern for the rest of the season. Coach Patterson believed in giving everyone a chance to play.

The Dick Bass era at Vallejo High School had arrived with the win over Lodi.

Vallejo High 21 Stockton 6

Dick Bass enjoyed another big night in leading the Apaches to a 21 to 6 victory over Stockton. Vallejo had lost four straight years to Stockton and this win was sweet. Dick Bass scored twice on runs of 4 and 64 yards. He carried 17 times for 162 yards and earned a 8.2 yards per carry average. He threw one pass for 40 yards to keep the Stockton defense honest and display his versatility. Dick now had 7 touchdowns in two games.

Stockton penetrated Vallejo territory only once in the final seconds of the first half. Stockton scored with two minutes remaining in the game. The Apaches scored the first time they got their hands on the ball when Johnny Eaton rushed for 34 yards and Bass 19 to set up the score. Bass took it over from the four by knifing into the end zone. Rodrigo converted the first of his three successful extra point attempts. On the drive for the third touchdown Eaton and

Bass ran and passed to get the ball to the eight and Don Rodrigo packed it in for the score.

Dick Bass had a great night as a runner, passer, receiver and decoy. Stockton had a good team, a big tough defensive minded bunch of brawlers. Adrian Vera the Stockton tackle told Ed, "he thought they were tougher but we were faster". Don Rodrigo was tremendous that night, blocking, tackling and smashing into middle of the brawlers. Rod loved knocking people down. Zunino was our punter and that night he punted a 45 yarder out of bounds on the three. The Apache linemen, who were outweighed by 25 pounds per man, manhandled the brawlers on defense and offense. Our defense started to show itself. Pete Kalamaras started to shine.

Now 2 and 0, we are feeling pretty good. We have beaten two good teams. Our offense and defense are coming together. We are ready for McClymonds.

Vallejo 27 McClymonds 6

A crowd of more than 5,000 watched the Apaches win a hard-fought contest with McClymonds 27 - 6. The visitors scored first and led at the half. The Apaches were out of sync and the McClymonds defense was worthy. The Apaches came back in the second half and took total control of the game, both on offense and defense. Vallejo marched to three touchdowns in the third quarter and added another in the fourth. The Apaches took the second half opening kickoff and rolled in six plays to score . Bass with a 43 yard kickoff return and three acrobatic runs got the ball to the 7 yard line and Rodrigo drove it into the end zone. Two minutes later, Johnny Eaton grabbed a punt on the midfield stripe and raced and danced 50 yards for another score. The blocking was devastating. Ed Sowash recalls that on Eaton's return, the Apaches knocked most of the McClymonds players to the ground hard. Still in the 3rd quarter, Dick Bass ground out a 57 yard masterpiece in six plays for a third touchdown in the busy third quarter. In the fourth quarter, Johnnie Eaton paved the way with a 49 yard run for the fourth and final score. We were back in sync and we had two great running backs.

McClymonds was late arriving and the game was delayed 32 minutes. They mouthed a little too much trash talking. Some of our players, DL in particular, became noticeably irritated as the McClymonds attitude made little sense. They had arrived late, then felt the need to trash talk. Definitely not cool.

Dick scores twice for a total of 9 TDs in three games. He ran inside the tackles for most of the night. He was playing sick with a severe cold. Rodrigo was injured in the first half but was more than ready for the second. Dick Bass and Don Rodrigo provided leadership by their example and their contrasting styles. Dick said little and Don said a little more but both were inspirational and respected by our teammates.

Pete Kalamaras, Ron Stover, Bernie Fleming, Ed Sowash and DL Hurd with his thundering kick-offs all made significant contributions to the win.

Next Friday night we host the Salinas Cowboys at Corbus Field.

Vallejo 35 Salinas 0

The Apaches walloped Salinas 35 to 0. In the words of Don Gleason "Salinas was sadly-outclassed," and implied maybe the game did not need to be played. True, but it was played.

Dick Bass ran for three touchdowns of 52, 19, and 98 yards in the first half. The 98 yard sprint down the field was a wonder to observe. Sowash and Cook opened the hole, Cameron led the play, Dick was in the Salinas backfield instantly, he went right at the safety, made one of his patented moves, the safety fell over his own feet and Bass was on his way to the end zone. Years later when Dick was a Pro with the Los Angeles Rams, Vince Lombardi opined that Dick Bass had more moves than a Swiss watch. The Salinas safety experienced one first hand that he might want to forget.

Don Rodrigo, Johnnie Eaton, Mark Cameron, Ron Stover, Tom Zunino and Cefius Johnson together forged three touchdowns. Ron Stover's leaping catch in the end zone for the touchdown was a highlight. Stover did it all that night, ferocious blocking, tackling and his impossible catch for the score. The starters played a little over a quarter in the first half and one minute of the second half. Reserves are getting opportunities to show their stuff. We are getting comfortable and having fun together.

Bob Sartwell, a standout at guard for the Cowboys and later a teammate of Dick and Ed at UOP, shared some kind words, that "the 53 Apaches were the best high school team we ever played." You guys had a lot, no a hell of a lot, of good players." Sartwell played opposite Pete and noted, "I got him once real good, but only once. He was an evasive little rascal."

Dick now had 12 touchdowns in four games.

We were now 4 and 0, and the reserves were getting significant playing time. 5,000 fans were in attendance.

Next stop Drake.

Note:

Jimmy Underhill, the Santa Rosa High School football coach, was one of the officials for the Salinas game. In five weeks, we would play the Santa Rosa Panthers for the title. He was getting a good look at who we were and what needed to be done to defeat us. He was also an official for NFL games, a real pro, football wise and very competitive. Underhill and Patterson were friends and played together at St. Marys College.

Vallejo 40 Drake 9

Dick Bass ran for five touchdowns and seemed unstoppable. Dick accumulated 186 yards in 11 carries for a 17 yard average per carry. The Apaches were in front by a 27 - 7 count at halftime and owned a 33 - 7 advantage after three periods. Nate Peterson, used mostly for blocking purposes, packed the ball for three straight plays and blasted over guard for the score. Nate gained 25 yards in his three packs.

The defense lead by Don Rodrigo and a dominant line throttled the Knights offense. Pete Kalamaras caused and recovered a fumble and spent most of the evening disrupting the Drake backfield. Bernie Fleming blocked a punt to set up the sixth and final tally.

Dick has scored 17 touchdowns in five games. 2,500 fans, a good contingent from Vallejo, were in attendance.

We are looking forward to facing Napa.

Note:

In the stands scouting us that night was Len Read, the Santa Rosa Panther half back who we would play against in the final game of the season. Coach Underhill had sent Len and a couple of his teammates to assess our team and get an idea of how to stop Dick. Len, at their next practice explained to his teammates the rule, "you only get one chance to get him, if you miss it is over." From that point on, they only practiced defense as the one way to beat us. Little did we know.

Vallejo 34 Napa 13

The Apaches soundly defeated Napa before a turn-out crowd of 7,500 excited football fans, the largest Vallejo grid turnout since the Vallejo JC - Compton clash in 1947. They came to see Dick Bass and the undefeated Apaches do their thing. They did. Dick put on a spectacular display of all his talents carrying the ball 24 times for 153 yards for 6.3 yards per carry and two touchdowns. His supporting cast were equally proficient. Don Rodrigo passed to Ron Stover for a 53 yard touchdown that was picture perfect. Stover got behind the defensive back, Rod threw a strike, and Stover raced to the end zone for the score. Rodrigo had a strong game both on offense and defense, besides the touchdown pass, he punched in two short yardage touchdowns. He led the defense that subdued Napa's offense and allowed a minus three yards.

Johnnie Eaton delivered the most spectacular play of the game. Napa intercepted a pass on their 30 yard line and the defender looked like he would go all the way. Eaton ran him down on the one yard line. They scored, we were inspired. Reserves got more playing time. Coach Patterson called the victory "a great display of team work."

Dick now has 19 touchdowns in 5 games. We are undefeated and ranked number 2 in Northern California.

Tamalpias is next on the schedule.

Vallejo 47 Tamalpais 13

Dick Bass smashed the all-time Vallejo High School individual scoring record with five touchdowns of 1, 65, 11, 40, and 81 yards. The 81 yard run was extraordinary and barely describable. Dick did it all, he sprinted, he spun, he stopped, escaped, one Tam tackler swore he disappeared. The 4,500 fans were screaming like crazy. Dick went into the end zone, dropped the ball and jogged to the conversion huddle and thanked everyone for their fine blocking. We loved blocking for Dick because we knew that he just might go all the way.

Ceifus Johnson, who had just joined the team, scored two touchdowns on his first two carries, one for 30 yards and the second for 28 yards. Yes, his first two carries were for touchdowns.

Our defense held Tamalpais to three first downs and no touchdowns from scrimmage. Kalamaras recovered a fumble, Tom Zunino intercepted a pass and Bill Wilson blocked a PAT and the Apache defense throttled Tamalpais' game plan.

Johnny Eaton broke his leg and was lost for the season. His loss was felt.

Dick Bass has scored 24 touchdowns and became the Vallejo High School all time touchdown leader.

St Vincent's of Vallejo is next.

Note:

Santa Rosa was thinking about our game in two weeks in a big way. Coach Underhill called Eddie Erdelatz, the head football coach at the United States Naval Academy for help. He was Erdelatz's high school coach. Jimmy Underhill Jr. told us this story. His dad was thinking a lot about the Vallejo game. He explained that his dad called Erdelatz and asked him if he would design a defense to stop our short punt offense and Dick Bass. Erdelatz agreed and he did indeed provide the scheme requested. This was serious game preparation.

Vallejo 82 St. Vincent's 0

Vallejo overwhelmed St. Vincents 82 to 0 in a game that should not have been scheduled or played. 4,000 spectators watched and wondered how this contest between two good teams could be so lopsided. St. Vincents had a good record winning 5-1-1 against worthy small school opponents. Before the game, Saints coach Everett Irish talked about the game this way, "we have one chance in a thousand and on paper can make a game of it." His players must have wondered how they got into this predicament, going up against a juggernaut led by Dick Bass.

Dick scored 6 touchdowns carried the ball 13 times and gained 226 yards for a 13.4 yards per carry.

Coach Patterson played ever man on the squad and could do little to hold the score down. At half time, the score was 31 to 0 and Coach did not send the starters back on the field. We watched the second half in street clothes.

The one bright spot for the Saints that eventing was Larry Patton's towering punts which averaged 53 yards in seven attempts.

Dick has 29 touchdowns. Tops in Northern California.

The Apaches are ranked number two in Northern California behind Sacramento High.

Santa Rosa is next and we will be playing for the North Bay League championship.

The Vallejo High School Marching Band set its own record in this game. They played the fight song after every touchdown. There were so many touchdowns scored the band got real creative and played the fight song in half time, fast time, slow time, waltz and Jazz style.

Note:

While we were trouncing St. Vincents, Santa Rosa was fighting for a tie with Analy, another small school opponent. Coach Underhill was so unsettled by his team's performance that he took them back to their gym for a 40 minute practice. He made the point clear they had to play better to beat Vallejo. Coach Underhill was on a mission and he would not be deterred. We were always on his mind.

8

VALLEJO 7 SANTA ROSA 7

T HE SANTA ROSA CONTEST was the segue from the '53 to the '54 season. Both teams were playing for the North Bay League title. In addition to the title, we were playing for something more abstract; we were reaching for a perfect season. On the other hand we believe, the Panthers just wanted to derail our team and the vaunted Dick Bass. After all the Panthers had humiliated the Apaches the year before 42 to 0. This was a football game that was of great importance for both teams.

Santa Rosa was the defending champion of the North Bay League. They had a winning record 6 wins and 2 ties. They had one of the top high school football coaches in Northern California in Jimmy Underhill and they were a group of solid football players lead by Len Read and Doug Camilli. They had a strategy and a scheme they thought would work and take the win. They were prepared and they were ready to play. Len Read put it this way, "we believed that if we could contain Dick Bass, we could beat you."

There was another factor beyond the control of man that would impact the game, the weather. The field was a hazard zone. The first game had been postponed a week because of a severe winter storm with thunder, lightning and torrential rain. The field was a shallow lake, unplayable and dangerous. The storm persisted and it continued to rain all week and there was still a light rain the night of the game. The lake had drained but the field and become a shallow bog. Mark Cameron described the field this way, 'when I put my hand down to get into a three point stance, my hand sunk into the mud up to my wrist." He went on to say, " Dick's speed and his ability to cut and change directions was severely restricted." This made Len Read's precept on how to stop Dick a little more achievable, "don't miss on your first attempt because you will not get a second." On the other hand, to their advantage, Len Read and Doug Camilli were built for these conditions, straight ahead power runners. It was a hell of a game.

Pundits continually claim before big games that offense wins games and defense wins championships. That night on that swampy field two great high school football teams played championship defense. Each team would start drives, move 30-40 yards and then peter out, aided by a slippery ball, on a slippery field, through our slipperier hands. Punts went awry giving both teams opportunities to score.

We scored first late in the 2nd quarter. After a Santa Rosa altered punt, we drove the ball 44 yards for the touchdown. It started when Rodrigo hit left tackle for nine yards to the Santa Rosa 35. Rodrigo took the ball again and made the first down to the Panther 31. The Panther's defense stiffened. We ran the ball three times and ended up with a fourth and four. Then Don Rodrigo lofted a sideline pass to Cameron for the first down on the Santa Rosa six. Dick ran it in on the next play for the touchdown. Rodrigo converted.

At half time, the locker room was all business. Coach Patterson was calm and direct, "keep your poise," "keep doing our assignments and no mistakes."

At the end of the third quarter, Santa Rosa put together their touchdown drive. A Tom Zunino punt to Len Read was returned to the Santa Rosa 40 yard line. The Panthers ran 13 running plays for 60 yards with Read taking it in from the one. Their attack was relentless with Read and Doug Camilli carrying the ball for short yardage on power plays. Game tied 7 to 7.

We were locked together in a tug of war with no one getting the advantage until the last minutes of the game. After a punt, the Panthers moved down the field until our defense stopped them on our thirty yard line. After another exchange of punts, we took possession on the 50 yard line with three and a half minutes remaining on the clock. It was our chance to go down the field and win the game. Dick darted and powered to the Santa Rosa 35. Bass and Rodrigo jammed for 5 yards to the 30 yard line. With one minute left, it was third and five and Don Rodrigo passed long to Stover, who took it out of the hands of two defenders on the Panther five. Dick bulled his way to the three. Fifteen seconds of play remained. We went for the field goal.

Don Rodrigo was our kicker. Doug Stone was the center and Mark Cameron the holder. Doug hiked the ball; Mark placed it and Rod kicked it through the posts for the win. Stop! There was an official time out called for an injured Panther player. Don would have to kick again. This time the ball was wide and hit the right pole and careened in or out depending on your bias. Unfortunately, the official on the field said out. No replay. Game over, a tie.

Coach Patterson was so "pissed" at the umpire's ruling he ran up to the Official's booth to appeal the call. We had never seen him so angry. Don left the field in tears. We were all sad and in disbelief. We felt as though we had lost the game. We did not like the feeling of losing or suffering a tie which felt the same. For us juniors this was an important learning, "losing," or in this case being held to a tie, was not going to happen again, no matter the circumstances.

In a very meaningful way, this game got us mentally ready to pursue the perfect season.

The Apaches were Co-Champions of the North Bay League.

Dick Bass scored one touchdown for a total of 31 for the season.

Dick was held to a net 86 yards on 20 carries. Dick recalled years later,"It's funny, but the Santa Rosa game is the one I remember....took a beating physically and did not win."

The Apaches were ranked number 2 in Northern California before this game and Santa Rosa was ranked number 11. The following week when the final standings were announced, we were ranked number 4 and Santa Rosa number 5.

The injury time out was and is still controversial. Santa Rosa had no time outs left at the end of the game. Bill Clarke and Mark Cameron are absolutely certain it was a trick play. Bill Clarke, whose assignment was to block the "injured" player, said "he just just flopped and started moaning." Mark Cameron to this day, remembers "vividly" seeing the "injured" Panther leave the field smiling. He did his job. In the words of Don Rodrigo, "we were robbed."

Of course the Panther view is quite the opposite. When Ed and I interviewed Jim Underhill Jr., he assured us that his Dad would never pull a trick play like that and Ed agreed. Len Read categorically affirmed that there was no trick play. He did not remember the injured Panther.

9

1953 SEASON IMPACT

THE '53 SEASON WAS an invaluable preparation for our final season at Vallejo High. A core group of us gained significant experience and were important contributors to the success of the '53 season. Dick Bass, Ron Stover and Bernie Fleming were starters from the onset of the season. Ed Sowash, Pete Kalamaras and DL Hurd emerged as starters by the end of the season. Dave Edington, Bill Wilson, Tom Zunnio and Dale Flowers were given more playing time as the season progressed. We played side by side with some very good football players who made us keenly aware of what it takes to win football games. Winning was burned into our football souls. We would take this attitude into the '54 season.

We acquired confidence in ourselves and in each other. Although we did not lose to Santa Rosa, the tie brought home the fact that we could be stopped. We gained a more realistic understanding about what it takes to win games. There was now an expectation that we could win every game. After all, we had the marvelous Dick Bass and we were the mighty Apaches.

We played with some truly outstanding high school football players in 1953. Johnny Eaton was the best example of how to be a great teammate. John was one of the most unselfish players on the team. He had to make room for Dick and he did it without a murmur of resentment. In the 1952 season, John was our starting tailback and he scored eleven touchdowns; in 1953, alternating with Dick, he scored three. John did whatever he needed to do to help us win. He did it all, blocked, passed, ran and tackled. Unselfishness is a big part of what makes teams great. We saw his unselfishness at play and he had our respect.

Mark Cameron, as mentioned earlier, was co-captain and a good all-around player. He had a knack for making big plays. We saw him as a leader. He was smart, confident, and a reassuring presence on the team.

Seniors Dick Tharp, Ron Cook, Doug Stone, Dennis Newman and Fred Gardner were tough and that toughness was a badge of honor. It was not blatant; it was just who they were as people and as football players. Toughness grows on you when you have to interact with people who thrive on it in practice every day. We embraced this attitude and carried it into the next year.

Don Rodrigo was our most valuable player, an honor he had received in his junior year as well.

He was the team leader and in a very real sense our coach on the field. He was one of those guys that leads by example. He played hard on every play and he expected the same from his teammates. Don was a student of Coach Simpson's style of play, discipline, toughness, conditioning and teamwork that were the ruling values. He knew the game and he was a bruising blocker, tackler and inside runner. Don was our connection to the Vallejo football tradition and an inspirational teammate.

We were prepared for the 1954 season.

10

1954 SEASON PREPARATION AND PRACTICES

AUGUST 23 WAS THE FIRST DAY of practice, and 100 young men were seated in the bleachers of Bottari Gym waiting for the coaches to address the team. Coach Patterson started off with a question, "How many of you senior's did not come out last year, please raise your hands?" and thirty did. Coach asked them to come down to the gym floor and he addressed the thirty candidates. He said, "Thank you for coming, but we will not be needing your services this year." The shock was felt throughout the gym. This gesture made it very clear to us that this was serious business, and he got our attention. His talk was short and sweet, "Don't be late, don't miss practice and do your job. Let's get our gear and get started." His message was clear and we took it to heart. The tone was set and we held to it for the season.

The first week was back to fundamentals of conditioning, blocking, tackling, ball drills and light hitting. We were an undefeated veteran team. The coaches knew, more or less, who the starters would be in what positions. The coaches were integrating the new players into the team. Our reserves were made up of many fine players and a few who were great, Bob Coronado and Norman Bass come to mind. We were loaded.

Coach Patterson would later say we were the best team he ever coached. He treated us like pros since he knew what we could do. He was getting us ready for the big dance. We worked on timing, working together and our focus. Then he gave us the test.

On Thursday of week two, Coach Patterson called us together and notified us that we were going to scrimmage the Vallejo Jr. College today. He smiled with his surprise announcement and our reaction. We were delighted and the adrenaline started to flow. They explained the rules of the controlled scrimmage. One team would start on the 40 yard line, and would continue until you were stopped or scored, then the other team got the ball. We scored 11 times and the JC scored once. We were into it. The scrimmage ended abruptly when out of frustration a few of the JC players switched from football to boxing. The scrimmage was stopped and we had passed the test. Patterson knew we were good and ready for the season.

Then Coach Patterson proffered another decision that would strengthen the team. An incident occurred during these first weeks of practice that was instrumental in defining ourselves as a team and as individuals. Coach Patterson went to Ed Sowash and explained that he had a serious team problem that he did not know how to deal with. Ed looked and sounded very concerned, and said, "I got real nervous, real nervous. What did I do?" Coach further explained that it was a racial problem, and Ed knew immediately it was serious. He told Coach he would talk to Dick about it and get back to him. The problem disappeared just like that. Today we would call this shared leadership then we called it friendship and we were not going let anything get in the way. We were Apaches.

In our interviews, it was noteworthy how many times the topic of race came up. It seemed that our cohort of friends felt that we seemed to get beyond it and race was not affecting our relationships. The interracial friendships were genuine and persist to this day. This speaks to the quality of our school and community leadership at that time.

1954 Practice—Jumping Jacks

11

THE SUPPORTING CAST

BEFORE WE GET INTO THE ROUGH STUFF, everyone knows true greatness always includes a supporting cast. We had the super fan and the pom pon girls, the cheerleaders, the marching band and the Vallejo fans.

The super fan is the person who is at every home game, a little quirky, noticeably noisy and loved by the home crowd and hated by the visitors. Clarke Millholland gave us the story of our super fan. Clark's good friend Cathy Giant asked him if he would volunteer to hand crank the fire siren after each touchdown. Clarke thought about it and said, "You know, help a friend out, get a little attention, have some fun and why not." He volunteered. He related to us, "In that moment, I did not think about how many touchdowns you guys would score. That was a lot of cranking. To this day, I still think my cranking arm looks a little different. But, without hesitation, I would do it again." We had our super fan.

Our pom pon girls were the best. They attended every game, constantly in synchronized motion, and supporting the cheerleaders on every cheer. They were unique. Sally Case explained why. "They made everything, their pom pons, their skirts and blouses and they created all of their own routines. The skirts were made of corduroy and their blouses were made from pajama tops." Quite stylish for the time. The skirts were four inches above the ankle. At that time, Lee Logan's dad was the manager of Crowley's department store and they got the Manager's discount on all their purchases. Sally, who still follows the evolvement of today's incarnation of the pom pon girls, thought out loud in our conversation and said, "I sort of wish we had been a little more risque." We agreed and they were still the greatest.

The cheerleaders were exceptional. There were four cheer leaders, Iva Swearingen, Jan Walton, Ronnie Ferrera and Maynard Willms. At that time, male cheerleaders were not permitted by the North Bay League. Maynard Willms recounted how they had to appeal to the NBL for a variance to the rule to be our cheerleaders. They were successful and received permission only for the coming year and then they would review the situation before making a final decision. Maynard sincerely believed that because we were the greatest football team in California it followed that our cheerleaders had to be pretty good too. The rule was changed and we had the first male cheerleaders in the North Bay League.

Our band stirred the emotions, no doubt about it. We warmed up together on the field, the band in the back of the end zone. Margret Cake would get them lined and tuned for the march to midfield and the National Anthem. Six majorettes with twirling batons led the parade. They led the celebration of every touchdown with creative renditions of our Fight Song. They played a lot of music and always found ways to highlight the artistry happening on the field with sound. In Margret's words, "They had a blast," and that energy was felt by everyone on and off the field.

In our conversations with contributors, it was often mentioned that our football team put Vallejo on the map. The stands overflowed with our classmates, our parents and Vallejo football fans who were proud and noisy. They came to see us play and give us their ever loving support. After all, we were their home grown product. The stands were full, the cheering intense and with the spectacular Dick Bass, the mighty Apaches did their thing.

When our supporting cast came together after a touchdown, it was special and we felt it. We can hardly imagine what opponents thought when they faced off with Vallejo.

Berkeley is our first contest.

Cheer Leaders

Pom Pon Girls

12

THE 1954 SEASON

THE BERKELEY YELLOWJACKETS were the reigning Alameda league champs and were led by Bob Sabilia, a high school All American center. All we knew is what Coach Patterson told us. They are a good football team. Let's get ready. He announced the lineup and then he said, 'keep your poise" and "let's go out there and play football." When we came down onto the field and heard our welcome, we knew, we were going to kick ass.

Vallejo 40 Berkeley 0

Our defense made it clear immediately to the Yellowjackets that it was going to be a long night. Our defense was smothering and Pete Kalamaras put on a show. Pete would be on all fours swiveling side to side and at snap the ball instantly dart into the line in whatever crack appeared, yes, that included going between the legs of the opponent. Pete was 5 feet 4 inches tall and 154 pounds and he struck like a lightening bolt. He was a big time "disrupter." Our fans loved Pete and his acrobatics on the field.

We scored late in the first quarter, with Dick capping a 70 yard drive with a 20 yard dash to the end zone. We broke the game open in the second quarter. We immediately drove 67 yards with Dick finishing the last 15 yards for the score.

After an almost blocked punt fell short, Tom Zunino threw a perfect 16 yard pass to Ron Stover for the touchdown. The next score came early in the third quarter when Dick delivered one of his classic 49 yard Houdini touchdowns runs. Behind fine blocking, Richard dodged and twisted, changed directions, changed speeds and when he appeared trapped, he disappears. The crowd went nuts, it was something to behold.

Bernie Fleming scored the last touchdown on a reverse going 40 yards untouched to the end zone, game over.

Our reserves took over and Bob Coronado ran for the last score. We always thought that one of the best teams we played was our reserves and they agreed. Norman put it this way, "when you guys were finished, it was our turn to play." Bob Coronado and Norman Bass would have been starters on any team we played. Our reserves assured the team that we would never miss a beat when they came in the game. They kept us sharp.

- The defense held Berkeley to 128 total yards.

- Dick Bass scored three touchdowns, gaining 185 yards on 16 carries for an average of 11.5 yards per carry.
- 5,000 in attendance.

Lodi is next on the schedule.

1954 VHS Offensive Starters

Vallejo 40 Lodi 7

This game got off on the wrong foot. It was hot in Lodi, it was steaming in the visitors locker room, temperature in the 100 degrees plus range. Coach Patterson told us we could continue dressing outside. We had our pregame meeting outside. He started with guidance, "we are going to take it easy, walk to the end zone, get loose, light work, let's go." DL and Pete led the team down on to the field. We had to walk the length of the field to the visitors end zone. The Lodi fans booed us, we could not believe it, a big mistake. We were ready to play.

Adding kindling to the fire, John Gionnoni, the Lodi coach, had called Dick a "powder puff runner," you can imagine what Dick was thinking. It brought a smile for sure and hard to imagine anyone calling him "powder puff." The Flames were going to feel the heat tonight.

In the first half, Dick Bass ran for two touchdowns and 104 yards in seven carries for a 14.9 yard average per carry in the first half. Gionnoni must have thought, "two touchdowns in seven attempts, that's a lot of puff."

The defense gave up one touchdown in the last 1:05 minutes of the game. Lodi was a very good team. They ended the season with 8 wins and 1 loss. At the end of the season, they were the San Joaquin-Sacramento Valley League champions and ranked 2nd in Northern California behind the Apaches. That one loss must have hurt them deeply. Why? Ed tells the story of making a recruiting trip to Lodi High School. While waiting for the Athletic Director, he was looking at the Lodi trophy case and saw the picture of the 1954 undefeated team. Yes, it said the 1954 undefeated league champions. We concluded that they only had one non-league game that year and it hurt. In the Lodi game, our defense stopped a great offense and our offense beat a great defense. We were in harmony.

Tom Zunino threw three touchdown passes, a 18 yard strike to Bernie Fleming, a 22 yard screen pass to Dick and a short pass to Stover. Stover made a move on the linebacker, took the pass and bowled over a defensive back for the touchdown. Tom now had four touchdown passes in two games. The short punt formation is not a passing style offense but our pass game is real good.

- In two games now the starters have not given up a touchdown.
- Dick has scored 7 touchdowns and he is the Northern California scoring leader.
- 5,000 thousand fans were in attendance.
- The Berkeley coach Fred Moffett was quoted in the *Oakland Tribune*, "Bass is the greatest running back I've ever seen."

Next McClymonds.

Ron Stover, Bernie Flemimg and Coach Thomas

Vallejo 47 McClymonds 6

McClymonds was a trash talking team. They were in 53 and they were that night the minute they got off the bus. D L had a friend on the team and they got into a little friendly talk. But there was some talk from other McClymonds players that had a little more bite, like "we're coming for you Bass," not cool, not cool at all. We heard Ed Sowash chanting, "Keep your poise men, keep your poise men." Ed was Coach Patterson's man on the field. Ed and Tom were co-captains and they went to mid-field for the coin toss. The general rule then and now is that you want to win the toss, get the ball, score first and gain a psychological advantage. This was true unless you wanted to make a statement. McClymonds won the toss and, to everyones surprise, decided to kick off to Dick Bass. A decision that was foolish and a little disrespectful. Ed and Tom came back to our kick off huddle and the unstated sentiment was for sure, "let's get things settled quickly."

Within two minutes, Tom Zunino and Dick Bass connected for a 40 yard touchdown play. The siren blared, the band belted out the fight song and the jumping and hollering started and would continue all night. DL launched one of his booming kickoffs and a McClymonds back caught it and headed for our sideline and Ron Stover hit him so hard that he was bent in half sideways and fumbled. Dave Edington recovered the fumble. Dick took an inside route behind Edington, Stover and Flowers for the score. In less than three minutes, the score was 14 - 0. We scored once more in the first quarter and followed through with touchdowns in every quarter.

The only noise heard on the field was coming from our fans, the place was jumping with joy.

Our passing game was on display that night, Tom had six completions and Dick had four accounting for 183 yards and two touchdowns. People sometimes forget that we had a balanced attack. We could move the ball on the ground and in the air. Our preferred mode of movement, of course, was on the ground.

The defense throttled McClymonds for the whole game. They gained 72 yards and their only score came in the last seconds of the fourth quarter. In three games, we had held three very good teams to one last second touchdown. The defensive line was fast, strong and down right miserly in giving up yardage. If the runner did slip through, he was met by DL Hurd and his menacing 6' 4" presence. We did not keep track of sacks or pressures at that time. All we know is that very little passing yardage was gained against us and one passing touchdown was allowed in nine games.

It should be noted that we did not platoon offense and defense; our starters played both ways. We took great pride in playing this way and we relished in the fine art of hard blocking and sure tackling.

- McClymonds ended their season as co-champions of the Oakland Athletic League. It takes a good team to come back from a shellacking.

- 6,000 were in attendance and our fans were spilling over to the visitors side of the field.
- Dick Bass has 12 touchdowns in three games.
- Tom Zunino has five touchdown passes in three games on a team that is predominantly a running team.
- The starters have not given up a touchdown.
- Don Fell made the *San Francisco Chronicle* team of the week.

Salinas is next.

Five Players with Coach Patterson

Vallejo 77 Salinas 12

Paul Abbott reported the game this way, "The quiet serenity of this farming community was shattered here yesterday when the powerful Vallejo High School Apache football team, sparked by amazing

Dick Bass' five touchdowns, humiliated the winless Salinas High Cowboys, 77-12, before 3,000 spectators." That is what happened pure and simple. Salinas was not a good football team. They had a few good players but the team was no match for the Apaches.

Our starters played a total of 15 minutes for the game. In that time, Dick Scored 5 touchdowns and ran for 285 yards on 9 carries for 31.7 average per carry. That is pretty scary when you think about it. What is even scarier was the hard hitting going on at the same time. The blocking on the way to those five touchdown runs was punishing. Dick helped his blockers; he would make moves setting the defender up for the best angle to be hit. We took great pride in our blocking and knocking people down for Dick. We had a mutual admiration society.

The reserves took over and they scored seven more touchdowns. Everybody got a chance to play and it was an eye-opener to see all the talent on our team. Bob Coronado returned a punt 73 yards for a touchdown. His speed and grace when running was a marvel to behold, a smooth operator. Norman Bass was on fire. He threw a perfect strike to Otis Grimble for a 48 yard touchdown play. Next possession he threw another perfect strike to Leon Wilson for 74 yards and a touchdown. He left the game and Mike Campas came in the and promptly tossed a 25 yard perfect pass to Clyde Huyck for a TD. The Salinas players must have been wondering when this would all end.

At the end of the game, several spectators came up to Coach Patterson to complain that they had come to see the vaunted Dick Bass in action and he only played one quarter.

Both Salinas touchdowns came at the end of each half. Salinas Assistant Coach Jack Fourcade was asked by a *Chronicle* reporter to give an adjective to best describe Vallejo, and we quote, "The adjective necessary to describe Richard Bass and his Vallejo power team does not exist." That is a fine compliment coming from a coach who had suffered a devastating defeat. We appreciated it.

That week the *San Francisco Chronicle* printed the Northern California high school football standings and the Vallejo Apaches were number one. Impressive wins over Berkeley and Lodi made it clear we had earned the ranking. We would remain there for the remainder of the season.

- Dick has scored 17 touchdowns and is the Northern California touchdown leader.
- Bill Wilson was selected to the Northern California defensive honor role.
- Four games and no touchdowns scored against the starters.
- Going home on the bus, we started clapping and stomping and looking forward to the dance. We loved to dance.

Next stop Drake

Vallejo 52 Drake 0

We were undefeated, ranked Number 1 in Northern California and we were playing before 7,000 zealous fans. It is hard to describe the feeling we had running on to the field and hearing our crowd noise, loud, boisterous and adoring. Intense excitement filled the place and we were going to play football.

The game started with a DL Hurd towering kick off and Drake started on their ten yard line; three plays later they punted. We got the ball at mid-field on our first series and Dick Bass raced and dodged 50 yards to score with a platoon of blockers clearing the way. It was immediately clear to everyone, we have a serious mismatch.

Don Gleason described Dick that night as "a blurred ghost, untouchable," and he was just that. He ran for four touchdowns, he carried the ball eight times and gained 274 yards for an average of 34.3 yards per carry. He was used only on two plays in the second half and gained 120 yards and a touchdown. "Intoxicating" is how Charlie Santiago described Dick's performance that night.

Our fans came to see us play and they were treated to an array of thrills. Bob Coronado made the longest run of the night, a 84 yard off tackle run for a touchdown. Bob was deceptively fast. We had team speed and so much more. We had attitude, and we expected win. We were not boastful; we were confident.

- No touchdown scored against the starters in five games. We took great pride and satisfaction in shutting down our opponents.
- Dick carried 8 Times for 395 yards for an average of 49.4 yards per carry, a truly remarkable performance.
- After five games, Dick has scored 21 touchdowns, gained 1,192 yards, on 69 carries for a 17.3 yards per carry.

Napa is next.

Rallies and Practices

Just to remind everyone that things went on between games that added to our success on game day. We practiced every school day and practiced started precisely at 3:30. The players would start practice without the coaches. Someone would yell let's get started and we would get going. Pete, Tom and DL liked to lead the drills. There was a little jive, good humor and quiet preparation, so when the coaches arrived we were ready for the game plan and fine tuning. Coaches treated us like pros and we responded.

The rallies before the games were highly emotional, the auditorium was packed, deafening cheers, bouncing pom pon girls, the upbeat band, literally "the whole banana" was there to get us all ready for the upcoming game. Coach Patterson would give a short talk, acknowledge the school community, express our appreciation for their support and remind us all that we were the Vallejo High School Apaches.

Vallejo 53 Napa 0

The Napa game gave everyone present an opportunity to see a great defensive team in action. The Apache defense had been dominant all season; but it moved into another dimension in the Napa game. The Big Red Machine moved as one to the ball and performed perfectly the plays you expect to see on defense: blocked kicks, interceptions, sacks, disruptions, fumble recoveries and hard clean tackling.

The defense started quick, the Napa quarterback Don Reeves went back to pass and was hit hard by Ron Stover and fumbled which led to a pushing and shoving match between Bill Wilson and Ed Sowash to get the ball. Wilson won and scored the touchdown.

Later in the first quarter, half back John Langenbach took a hand off and was hit by Sowash, fumbled, and Bill Wilson recovered and we scored.

Steve Galios took over at quarterback for Napa and was immediately pressured by the line and in desperation shoveled a pass which was intercepted by Dave Edington who took it for the touchdown. In another spectacular play, Dick intercepted a Galios pass in the end zone and ran 102 yards for a touchdown. It was called back because of a clipping penalty. In another punting situation, there was a full on line charge toward the kicker and we still do not know who blocked the kick; it was clear that if the punt was not blocked, we would have received a roughing the kicker penalty. There was a pile of players around the kicker and the ball was loose and Wilson recovered again.

Our fans loved our defense and Pete was a favorite. When he made one of his plays, there was literally a unique roar that would come from the stands. It was Pete's roar, pure and loud. We learned how to play team defense in Junior High and we executed it with skill, commitment and passion.

Our offense was humming. Dick Bass registered four touchdowns on runs of 20, 34, and 81 yards. The 81 yard run contained everything; Dick faked a pass and then headed up field. The fake caused a fatal hesitation by the Napa defenders. Dick took off, changed speeds, used his blockers, broke a tackle and found daylight. A 81 yard masterpiece was delivered to the 6,000 astounded fans. It was vintage Dick Bass. The other two offensive touchdowns were scored by DL Hurd and Dale Flowers. DL was becoming a trash talker as the season progressed; that night he started trash talking the all NBL tackle Jack Piper. DL would say to Piper, "Here we come Piper," and that's where we would go. In the huddle, Ed complained, "DL, I have to block this guy." DL smiled and kept talking to Piper, even when we were going to some other hole. Flowers' touchdown, on the other hand, is a little more involved. Flowers tells the story this way, " Here I am the other half back on the highest scoring high school football team ever for nine games. Well, my numbers are modest. I carried the ball three times, fumbled once, scored once and got the ball by mistake. All in one game, the Napa game." He is proud of those stats.

- Vallejo is ranked number 1 in the Northern California standings for the second week.
- No touchdowns scored against the starters.
- Bill Wilson made the Northern California defensive honor role for the second time.
- The defense scored two touchdowns.
- In six games, Dick Bass has scored 25 touchdowns and gained 1,446 yards. More sports reporters are coming to games and writing stories about Dick Bass and the Apaches.

Tamalpais is next.

The Defense

Our defense was exceptional. Only two touchdowns scored against the starters. Speed was the hallmark of our defense. We played team defense. Few running backs ever got into our backfield. Most times they were stopped before they got to the line of scrimmage, if they got through the line, there stood DL in all his fearsome self; it was over quickly. Hard tackles and swarming defense were the norm.

Our pass defense was the rush of the line. Few passes were complete and none for long yardage. One can only imagine that there might be a receiver who could get behind Richard. It never happened.

Flowers vividly recalls a big fast receiver coming into his area of responsibility and before his fear became a reality, he heard the roar of the crowd and our line had tracked a passer to the turf.

No one kept track of fumbles, three and outs, sacks, pressures or disruptions. We expected those plays on every snap. They occurred often and they were a source of many offensive advantages. We did not think you could score against us. We had complete confidence in each other to make certain our opponents would be stopped.

We have to give credit to Coach Thomas who was a believer in defense and our line coach. Like all of our coaches, he was a Vallejo product, came to Vallejo from Texas as a child, attended Vallejo Junior High, Vallejo High and Vallejo JC. He lettered in football, basketball and track, and in 1936 he was a member of Vallejo High's first undefeated football team. Coach Thomas was easy going, even tempered, a good communicator and an excellent teacher. Dave Grabest described one lesson Coach Thomas gave on defensive play, "He taught me how to move in minute detail from my stance to get to the ball. I remember the lesson to this day." On defense, his mantra was, "Watch the ball, that is where you want to be." When you think about what our front line accomplished, on offense and defense, they were exceptional and very well coached.

DAVE EDINGTON, DON FELL AND DALE FLOWERS

Vallejo 87 Tamalpais 25

As we demolished Tamalpais, we were met by Larry "Squeaky" Davis, the Tamalpais fullback who put on a show of his own. Davis scored three touchdowns on runs of 66, 61 and 43 yards and, most importantly, made a devastating block that knocked Dick and Tom to the ground that allowed the first passing touchdown against the starters. That touchdown was the first touchdown scored against the starters in seven games. A truly great performance by the junior fullback. Larry Davis got our admiration and respect that night. The dude had heart and talent.

After Larry Davis, there was no defense to stop our offense with Dick literally running free. Bass made five touchdowns on 12 carries, totaling 174 yards for an average of 14.5 yards per carry. The offense was now in another dimension. We believed that every time Dick got the ball we were going for the touchdown, no matter where we were on the field.

Ron Stover caught two touchdown passes, caused a fumble, blocked a punt and made the recovery. One reporter commented, "We have seen two of the best high school football players in California tonight, Dick Bass and Ron Stover."

Coach Patterson kept the starters in the first period and substituted every last man before half time. The starters played the third quarter and the first minutes of the fourth quarter. It was the most action the starting eleven had seen this season. You got to hand it to "Squeaky."

- We have a new term being used by the Bay Area football pundits, "Basstistics." 97 carries, 1,517 yards gain for a 15.6 average for the season, 30 touchdowns, 30 conversions and most points scored, 210 points.
- Ron Stover made the Northern California Prep defensive honor role.

- The Vallejo Apaches are number one in Northern California and now mentioned as the top team in California.

Next Riordan.

Vallejo 52 Riordan 0

The banner in the *San Francisco Chronicle* read "Riordan 'STOPS' Dick Bass, but bows to Vallejo, 52-0. Before the game, Head Coach Visco Grgich vowed Riordan would stop Dick Bass. Coach Grgich played for the 49ers for seven years and was know as a fiery, tough, two way linemen. Riordan set out to do one thing, stop Dick. They came up with a weird defense that had one to three down linemen and the rest you could only call "bassmen." This was humorous, you can imagine, eight to ten players following Dick around all night.

That opened the barn door for D.L. Hurd and he came charging onto the field breaking tackles and running over people for three touchdowns. Unlike Dick who would dance, make a move and disappear, DL preferred dance, make a move and run through you. With our love of blocking and DL's devastating running, our ground game did not lose a beat. Coach Grgich must have wondered and admired what he had unleashed.

Riordan started the game with a booming kick right to Dick. Was this part of their game plan or was it just a foolish mistake. Dick responded with another extraordinary 88 run for a touchdown. The harmony between Dick and his blockers was perfect. He ran into the end zone untouched. 8,000 football fans went bananas. The siren screamed, the fight song resounded and our fans were in the game and whooping it up.

DL scored twice on runs and caught a 19 yard pass from Dick for his third touchdown. With DL leading the charge, we scored on every possession, no punts. The reserves kept the offense moving and we scored in every quarter, 20 points in the fourth. Norman Bass scored twice and Bill Clarke and Roy Adams each scored.

The Apaches defense was stout, shutting down the run and making three interceptions. One interception by Dick included a 78 yard spectacular broken field return for a touchdown.

- Vallejo is the number one high school football team in Northern California.
- Riordan held Bass to 64 yards rushing on 16 carries for a 4.0 average.
- Dick Bass is the Northern California scoring leader with 223 points.
- Don Fell was selected to the Northern California Team of the Week.

We close the season next Friday against Santa Rosa.

We are starting to sense that this drama is about to come to an end. No one talks about it. It is more like feeling that you cannot deny. We are approaching a perfect season and the end of one of the most important experiences of our lives.

Vallejo 39 Santa Rosa 7

This was our final game together and we were playing the Santa Rosa Panthers for the NBL Championship. We did not forget the infamous 7 to 7 tie last year, the one blemish on a perfect high school football careers of Dick Bass, Ed Sowash and DL Hurd. They delivered their best games and led the charge. We were the Apaches and we were going to play football before 11,000 football fans. It was exciting and it would be memorable.

Ed's adrenaline was in full throttle. He was in on every tackle on every kick off, he recovered a fumble, caused a fumble, opened holes, blocked and recovered a punt. He did it all. One of his teammates swears he was growling every time he got into a four point stance. Ed believes that his performance that night assured him a football scholarship to University of Pacific.

DL was central to the defense and the offense that night, he set the tone, this was how we were going to play. We all joined in and played together like a fine Swiss watch.

This was Dick's last dance and did he dance. He scored five touchdowns and carried 24 times for 270 yards 11.7 average per rushing try. We find it impossible to describe how Dick Bass moved on the football field. You had to see it to believe it. He was 17, in perfect condition, with true instincts and a deep connection to the game. We were teammates and friends and we loved playing together.

When we got in the kickoff huddle and put our hands together, there was electricity in the air, this was our last game together, we knew it and we were going to finish it with elan. When we broke the huddle, the ovation was thundering. It was time for the Apaches to do their thing and we played.

Looking back, we might have been a little over hyped. We made simple mistakes that nullified two touchdowns. One was a 98 yard run by Dick incorporating most of his moves, and he stood in the end zone slightly peeved by the penalty, but only for a nano second. The noise from our fans was deafening. We do not think our fans really cared if this touchdown was denied, what mattered was that Dick gave us all another remarkable memory to be cherished until this day.

The game ended, the season was over and Dick was honored by in a brief ceremony where he received an All American sweater and invited to play in the annual National All Star game the following summer in Memphis, Tennessee.

Dick Bass and Coach Bob Patterson were hoisted on teammates shoulders and carried once around the field to the sound of joyous appreciation. It was a perfect end to a perfect season. *Sports*

Illustrated proclaimed Dick Bass the top running back in America that year and the Vallejo High School Apaches one of the top teams, if not the top team in America.

- Dick Bass in nine games gained 1,964 net yards for a 14.8 average per carry with 37 touchdowns and 256 points.
- The Apaches gained 4,617 yards averaging 513 yards per game and scored 488 points for an average of 54.2 points per game and 75 touchdowns.
- The Vallejo Apaches were the undisputed North Bay League Champions and selected the top team in Northern California.

The Locker Room

The locker room after the game was packed with press and quests, Jimmy Underhill, the Santa Rosa Coach, Milt Axt, the Poly San Francisco Coach and John Rhode, a University of Pacific assistant coach.

Coach Patterson went around the locker room congratulating players, mostly seniors. He gave us his closing comments. In his usual brief, direct and sincere manner, he said, "The whole team played outstandingly tonight and for that matter throughout the entire season. It has been a pleasure to coach such a group."

We don't remember if we did a hip-hip-hooray or raucous shouting; we could have done both. Anyway, we were going to the dance and we loved to dance.

1954 VALLEJO HIGH SCHOOL FOOTBALL TEAM

13

DICK BASS THE PERSON

W E ALL KNOW OF HIS athletic feats and what he could do on the football field. He was a great athlete, very fast and he had 3 speeds, fast, faster and faster yet. He could change direction in a split second, he could cut on a dime and give you a nickel change. He had eyes that could see behind him, great peripheral vision. He had great acceleration, and he was tough and could deliver a blow when he had too.

He was great in many sports, football, basketball, baseball, boxing and track, but football was his game. He could always take it to the next level in high school, college, and as a professional.

He should be in the NFL Hall of Fame.

But we want to talk about Richard the person. What was he like when he was not in a uniform. What was he like as a friend, teammate, classmate or just a person of interest. Here are the thoughts of family and friends who knew him, in their own words.

Dorothy Bass Atkins

To the outside world Dick was a hero and an outstanding athletic. To me he was a hero because he was the best brother you could have.

As our older brother he was expected to look after Norman and I. He seemed to take on that responsibility as a badge of honor and he kept an eye on both of us throughout our lives. The things that I loved and cherished about him was his kindness and his world view. For as long as I can remember Dick looked after me and encouraged me to always be brave and follow my own dreams.

Throughout his life and career, he phoned me daily to just talk about things that interested us together. He was humble about his talents but proud of his intellect. There was a gentle spirit about my brother in the way he could make people feel good about themselves. He had an ability to connect to people of all circumstances with great respect. Dick was ahead of his time.

His love of travel and different cultures played a large role in the way he connected with people. I have always wanted the story about my brother to include his character and his humanity. Plus his sense of humor always could change a situation from gloomy to great. I am honored to have been his sister and consider it a privilege to know that we both touched each others lives so immensely and that he touched the world in the way he lived his.

Norman Bass

Dick never told people he played for the Rams, or what he did for a living. He was not a bragger. He was very generous, and he would give people the shirt off his back. This person in the neighborhood, we will call him David, Dick gave him several pair of dress pants, they were too short, but he wore them anyway.

Dick gave nick names to everyone. He called my son Louis, as in Joe Louis, because he was always punching the bag. He called me "Coach," because I was always telling people how they should do things.

The Rams had a big awards dinner at the Hollywood Palladium and everyone was in tuxedos. Dick came in a Safari outfit leading a small elephant he had rented just for the entrance.

At one point in our lives, we lived together in L.A., Dick, Norman, and Norm III. We had fun, there was much laughter. One day I came home from work and Richard was in the street playing ball with the kids, at least 15 of them, and Dick goaded me into kicking the ball. I hit it just right and put it into the next county. He went into the house.

Richard Pryor and Dick were friends. Pryor thought that Dick was a very funny guy. Dick always gave credit to his teammates, His motto was, "Just play, don't run your mouth, just play." We were very close, he has been gone a long time, but I feel that he is still here. He was a great brother.

Bill Moore

I graduated from Vallejo High School in June of 1954, and played on the 1952 and 1953 football teams. This story relates to the 1954 season. During the 1953 season I was 16 years old and had not grown into my body. Coach Patterson did not discourage kids from playing though they often, like myself, played more from desire than physical ability.

The "however" here is that we produced a very successful team. The team's success centered on the exceptional skills of Dick Bass. I went from Vallejo to Menlo College for my first two years of college. I grew and matured a lot over the ensuing year and earned myself a role on a very successful J.C. team. This was the 1954 season. The Vallejo High Apaches of 1954 made national headlines during their very successful season. Now, as we (Menlo) approached the game in Vallejo, there was obvious team chatter about Corbus Field being the province of the Dick Bass phenom.

The real essence of this story is to shine a light on the wonderful, lasting essence of the Dick Bass personality. At the end of our game (which we won 20-12) as we filed under the stadium, I saw a cluster of students facing down our line as we moved toward our locker room. We got closer and I saw that Dick Bass was at the lead of this group. As I approached, Dick stepped forward, put out his hand for only me to shake and said "Nice game Bill." It soon registered that he was waiting there, with his pals, specifically to see me. I wouldn't have known that he even knew who I was, having been so far down the roster the previous year. As I came into the locker room, one of our lineman, said is that Dick Bass? and gave me a jaw drop when I said "Yes, I played with him last year." Now it has come to me, in retrospect, that gesture by Dick actually marked a turn-around in my life, socially and emotionally. It started as an elevated status with my teammates. Menlo was state JC co-champs that year (all wins, one tie). I played no more football after the two seasons I had at Menlo, but I will never forget that night.

Gent Davis

Gent directed two signs and field dedications in the memory of Dick Bass, and a walk of fame on the

High School front lawn in his memory. Gent had great admiration for Richard Bass, and he listed seven points that make up who Dick Bass was as a person.

He was low keyed and he controlled the situation. He had sensitivity to incarcerated people like the CYA and The California Correction facilities, which he visited many times. He was never one to brag, about sports, or setting records. He would always put the spotlight on others who came before him. He had respect (Aretha Franklin) for the other guy and he gained their respect as a person. He was streetwise (smarts), like when his father was telling him to stay away from the rift raft; he was already doing that. He was trustworthy. If he said something on Monday, it was the same on Wednesday and Friday. He was a person you could count on, a money in the bank type of person. He was a great friend.

Bob Coronado

We had a very good relationship, a long relationship. We played together in four sports at Vallejo High School: Football, Basketball, Baseball and Track.

We were the only 4 sport letter winners in the School. I saw Dick box as a young man. He was good, but he was good at everything. We played together at Pacific in football and baseball, then against each other in the NFL. He was with the Rams. and I was with the Steelers.

In my second season we were to play the Rams in Los Angeles, and I was looking forward to making the trip west to play against my friend Dick Bass, but two weeks before the game I broke my ankle and was out for several weeks and did not travel to Los Angeles.

I knew the whole family, wonderful family. They supported all the teams at Vallejo High. They were great people.

D. L. Hurd

Richard was a great person to be around. He would take care of people. He was the first in our group to have a car. He would pick us up to go to practice and then take us home. We all lived in Chabot and near each other. After Saturday practices we would come to my house and eat peanut-butter sandwiches on the porch, and talk about our day at practice. He always had a smile on his face. And he always had something nice to say about the opposing team players. He could get along with anyone and everyone. He had a great sense of humor and fun to be around. He was a great teammate and a great friend.

Ed Sowash

Richard and I were team mates for over 10 years - Peanut League, Jr. High, Sr. High and five years of College. "We were teammates for 10 years, but friends for Life."

He was a fun-loving guy, great sense of humor. He always would thank his blockers after a great run, "great blocking guys." He was appreciative of your help and told you so. He would always introduce me to his friends in L.A. as his help in High School and in College. That's what he called those who blocked for him, "his help." After he retired, we would call each other just to see how the other was doing. You OK? What are you up to? He was always true to his word, dependable. I was in Vallejo teaching and coaching at Hogan High School and just finished a class and went to my desk and who appears at the door, Richard. I said "what are you doing here?," "Oh! I was just speaking in Napa and was on my way to the airport, and thought that I would stop by and say hello. How are you doing?" He would do that, If he liked you, you were family. He was honest, always had a positive attitude and fun loving. He was a unique individual. He was a great friend.

Clark Millholland

I met Dick Bass when we played together on the same baseball team in the Peanut League (Pre Little League) in Vallejo. Dick was our catcher, and our best player. I was amazed that with all that gear on he could beat the hitter down to first base to back up the throw. He always encouraged everyone with positive comments. He was a great team mate.

In high school we were team mates again this time on the Vallejo High School Basketball Team. I remember after a game at Drake High School we were getting on the bus to go home when Dick spotted a canteen about two blocks away. We had a few minutes before the bus was to leave, so he said, "let's run down real fast and get something to eat." My first thought was I am going to run real fast with a guy that runs the 100 yard dash in 9.5 seconds. If he put 100 pounds on his back, he would still beat me by a block. As we were waiting to order, four Drake girls came up and asked for his autograph. I had never seen high school students ask another high school student for an autograph. Then clever Dick, in order to get his food first, told the girls they should get my autograph, because I was famous too. As I was signing autographs Dick got his order and ran back to the bus. I ended up getting chewed out by our coach for being late to the bus. He was a great friend.

Reflections

Above are reflections that we believe start to capture the essence of who Dick Bass was as a person. In our interviews," we were struck by how many of our classmates and teammates were touched in a positive way by Dick the person. He was famous and a hero in high school. No matter, when you were with him, you knew he was just as interested in you as you were in him. Dorothy Bass described her brother as a Renaissance man, looking back today, we can see he was well on his way when we were together in Vallejo.

14

LAST THOUGHTS

WHEN WE DECIDED TO TELL this story about the 1954 Apaches perfect season, we asked our contributors what they thought about why we were such great team. Everyone had an opinion. Edie Giant put it best, "You were so close to each other and functioned like a well-oiled sewing machine." Willis McJunkin said, "You were all such great athletes." Norman Bass proclaimed, "We were a unique group of characters," with the emphasis of the word *character*. Dave Grabest thought our system was simple, easy to learn and easy to implement. And more...It could have just been one of those times when everything just comes together. There were a lot of great athletics around Vallejo High School at that time, Dick Hegeman, Bobbie Lorentz, Augie Garrido, Richie Williams, Gent Davis and others. All we really know for sure is that we had one incredible experience that still speaks to our souls.

15

HALL OF FAME TEAMMATES

Below are the Vallejo Hall of Fame biographies of our key players and Coaches Patterson and Thomas. We think their athletic accomplishments further illustrates why the 1954 Apaches were a great high school football team.

Dick Bass

Sports Illustrated once called Dick Bass the hottest high school football player in the nation and what he did in his two years as the record-shattering left halfback for the 1953 and 1954 Vallejo High School Apaches proved they were right.

Bass' career totals for the Apaches may never be broken; 3690 yards per carry average. With 68 touchdowns and 34 conversions, Bass amazed a staggering 442 points in only 18 games.

Bass was a dangerous running back and anytime he touched the football fireworks were soon to follow. In one game, he returned the opening kickoff 88 yards for his first touchdown followed by a 55 yard punt return for his second, then raced 78 yards on a pass interception for a third score and, just to finish off the evening, he threw a 12 yard touchdown pass. In short, he did it all.

Football was not the only sport at which Bass excelled. As a track star, he ran the 100 yard in 9.8 seconds, he was Vallejo's amateur welterweight boxing champion, and he played in the East-West High School All-Star Baseball series in New York City.

Coming out of Vallejo High School with the state high school football scoring record and with high school All-American status, Bass became the most sought after high school prospect in the country. He was considered by many as the finest freshman running back in the nation while playing for the College of the Pacific Tigers and during his junior year in 1958, Bass became the second player in college football history to win the NCAA triple crown by leading the nation in rushing with 1,361 yards, scoring with 116 points, and total offense with 1,440 yards. In 1958, Bass had the distinction of being the first college junior ever selected in the first round by the NFL when he was drafted by the Los Angeles Rams.

A two-time college All American, Bass finished his collegiate career in 1959 by playing for the College All-Stars against the NFL World Champion Baltimore Colts.

During his 10 year career with the Rams, Bass was a two-time 1,000 yard rusher, appeared in three Pro Bowls, voted the NFL's Comeback Player of the

Year, and upon his retirement in 1969, was the Rams all-time leading rusher.

As an All-American in high school, All-American and Triple Crown winner in college, and Pro Bowl running back in the NFL, Dick Bass is considered by many to be Vallejo's greatest athlete.

Norman Bass

Norm Bass was the first African-American athlete to compete in two professional sports. A graduate of Vallejo High, Bass pitched for the Kansas City A's for three seasons and in 1964 he was a walk-on at a Denver Bronco's tryout where he made the team as their starting safety.

However, the road to athletic stardom was painful as devastating arthritis took away Bass' athletic dreams. Thinking his athletic career was over, his outlook toward sports turned bitter for more than 15 years. He refused to attend games or talk to his former teammates.

Today however, all of that has changed. After picking up a ping pong paddle to compete against a young man for fun, (he easily defeated the youngster) Norm was hooked. He soon discovered a table tennis club and started playing competitively.

In his youth, table tennis was something he played at the local recreation center on Amador Street. Bass became an extraordinary table tennis player hitting the tournament circuit in Las Vegas,

Florida, and Sydney Australia for the Paralympics. Bass competes in the Class 7 Division (disabled players able to stand) and, for a time, was ranked seventh in the world.

Energized by his competitive spirit, Norm continues to compete throughout the world. In 2002 U.S. Open in Florida, Bass won two silver and one bronze medal. That same year at the Pan-American Championships in Argentina, he won the gold. He has traveled to Hungary.

Today, more than 40 years after premature arthritis put an end to his professional athletic career, Bass shows no signs of slowing down. His son, Norm Bass III, has written a biography about his father that has piqued the interest of television producers. As a loving father and grandfather, Bass continues to receive plenty of encouragement from his family to keep on going and there is no doubt, he will.

D.L. Hurd

Greatness is defined in many ways. Some look at individual statistics. Others look at accomplishments on a team level. Still others feel the main qualification for entrance into any sports Hall of Fame should be championships and championships alone. D.L. Hurd, in that case, may be overqualified. From his sophomore year until the day he left college, Hurd played on 18 championship teams, including seven in baseball, six in football and five in basketball. Five of those titles came while a member of the Vallejo High School Apaches sports teams. Between 1953 and 1954 Hurd and his teammates won two North Bay League football titles, two NBL basketball titles and one baseball title. Along the way, Hurd was selected All-North Bay in football and basketball as well as earning All North Coast and All Northern California High School Basketball honors.

The kid could play. Hurd took his winning ways to Vallejo Junior College, where the Redskins won five more conference titles, including Coast Conference championships in football, baseball and basketball.

The 6-foot-3 Hurd averaged 19 points per game in basketball, and was considered one of the toughest rebounders in the league. Named All-Coast Conference and All-Northern California Junior College, Hurd led the Redskins to a second place finish in the State Junior College Basketball Championships.

His all-league honors weren't limited to basketball, as Hurd – a hard-hitting first baseman – was named All-Coast Conference and All-Northern California Junior College in baseball as well.

After finishing up at Vallejo JC, Hurd transferred to Gonzaga University, where – naturally – he won championships on the baseball and basketball teams.

Hurd finished his collegiate career at San Francisco State University, leading the Gators to a conference title in football. He was drafted by the Baltimore Colts in 1963 as an end – one of five members of the 1954 Vallejo High School football team to sign NFL contracts.

Following the completion of his professional athletic career, Hurd went on to a 35-year career at the Solano County Probation Department, working at Juvenile Hall. He was elected to the Solano Community College Sports Hall of Fame in 1995 for his exploits on the football field during the 1956 and 1957 seasons.

Bob Coronado

Whenever the conversation turns to who were some of the great athletes to come out of Vallejo High School, one name that always seems to rise to the top of the list, Bob Coronado of the graduating class of 1955. Regarded by many as one of the most talented and best all-around athletes, Coronado could do it all.

As a wide receiver and tailback with the famous 1954 Apache football team, Coronado helped the 9-0 Apaches to the North Bay League championship by scoring 12 touchdowns. But football wasn't his only sport. He was the starting power forward on the Apache basketball team and earned all-league honors by pitching 3 no-hitters and a couple of one-hitters for the championship Apache baseball team. If that wasn't enough, Coronado ran the 220 on the track team, topped 23 feet in the broad jump and would destroy the school record in the half-mile. In his senior year, Coronado helped the Apaches win 4 North Bay League Championships in four different sports. Coronado was also one of the five members of the 1954 Apache football team to be drafted by the NFL.

Following graduation from Vallejo High, Coronado, along with three of his Apache team-mates, enrolled on the campus of the College of the Pacific in Stockton, where Bob would serve as a wide receiver for the Tigers for the next four years.

After his college career, Coronado was drafted in 1959 by the Chicago Bears. The 6 foot2 inch, 180 pound speedster was also chosen to play in the College All-Star game - a game in which he caught 4 passes against the NFL Champion Baltimore Colts. Reporting to the Chicago Bears training camp, Bears Head Coach George (Papa Bear) Halas, said of Coronado, "This Coronado kid is good. He's got great hands. He's only the second receiver I've ever seen in 35 years, who's been able to catch the ball without you hearing the ball hit the hands." But as fate would have it, after just a couple of weeks in training camp and with Coronado scheduled to make the Bears opening day roster, Uncle Sam came calling and Coronado was off to serve the next two years in the Army. Staying in shape during his army days by running track and cross-country, Coronado would learn upon his discharge from the service that he had been traded to the Pittsburgh Steelers. Catching a 50 yard touchdown pass in his first pre-season game, it didn't take long for the Steeler organization to realize that they had the receiver they needed. Named to the Steelers starting offensive lineup as a rookie, Coronado's career was set to take off.

In a light workout in preparation for a game against the Dallas Cowboys, on an old poorly maintained high school field, which the Steelers used as their training camp, Coronado was running a pass-pattern and with his arms extended and his eyes on the pass, he stepped in a hole. Within the blink of an eye, his career was over. With a dislocated and fractured ankle, Bob Coronado would never play again. With this untimely career-shattering injury, no one will ever know just how great Coronado's professional career would have been. Former *Vallejo Times Herald* sports editor Dave Beronio probably said it best. "With his speed and his pass catching abilities, he would have been one of the best." And that's the way Vallejoans think of Bob Coronado, he was one of the best.

Tom Zunino

When Tom Zunino began his coaching career at Vacaville High School as a 23 year old assistant football coach in 1960, little did he know that his new career would span nearly four decades and include a legacy of success unmatched anywhere in Northern California.

Growing up in Vallejo, Zunino started his athletic participation at the young age of nine. From this early age through junior college, Tom would have the opportunity to learn how to play football, baseball and basketball from six future Vallejo Sports Hall of Fame coaches.

As a senior at Vallejo High School Zunino was the starting quarterback on the famous 1954 Apache football team. With Zunino calling the signals, the Apaches would win the North Bay League championship with a 9-0 record and outscore their opponents 488-57.

Following graduation from Vallejo High, Tom took his talents to the campus of Vallejo Jr. College where he quarterbacked the Redskins to a league championship. Regarded as one of the top Jr. College passers and field generals in Northern California, Zunino also won all league honors as a shortstop on the league champion Redskins baseball team. Following his graduation from Sacramento State and a stint in the U. S. Air Force, Zunino signed on as the assistant football coach with the Vacaville High School Bulldogs.

A year later looking to play pro ball and going into the family business during the off season, Zunino would turn down offers of pro contracts from both the Oakland Raiders and the Boston Red

Sox's. He was also offered the dual jobs of athletic director and head football coach for Vacaville High.

Over the next 37 years as head coach, Coach 'Z' as he is known, would post a record of 215 wins and 9 league championships. In addition, Coach 'Z' is one of 16 coaches in California high school history to win more than 200 football games and one of only 9 to win more than 200 at the same school. Over the years Coach 'Z' has also coached wrestling, basketball, baseball, track and golf.

Named the Sac-Joaquin Athletic Director of the Year from 1985–1987, Zunino was also named the State Athletic Director's Association A D of the Year in 1988 and the California Coaches A D of the Year in 1989.

Zunino however, draws the most satisfaction from Vacaville High's dominance of the Monticello Empire League. Since 1976, when the league was formed, the Bulldogs have won the School of the Year award 20 times including 10 years in a row from 1982–1991. The award is a point system based on the teams (both boy and girls) league records each year.

In addition to being elected to both the Solano Community College and Sacramento State Sports Hall of Fames, in September of 2005, the football facility at Vacaville High School was renamed Tom Zunino Stadium.

Asked about his legacy upon his retirement, Zunino said, "I believe I will be forgotten in a very short time." After a long and illustrious career, that might be the only thing he's gotten wrong.

Ed Sowash

Whether it was on the football field or the baseball diamond, Ed Sowash is considered by many to be one of the best athletes to ever come out of Vallejo. Born in St. Louis, Missouri, Sowash at the young age of seven would move with his family to Vallejo in 1943, and it was at this time he would develop a passion for sports and recreation by participating in all the programs offered by the Greater Vallejo Recreation District.

Sowash first became interested in playing football when he enrolled as a 9th grader at Hogan Jr. High School. Learning under head coach Mal Simpson, Sowash quickly started to show his skills as he would win All- City football honors for the next two years.

Moving over to the Vallejo High School campus as a junior, Sowash continued his dominance on the gridiron for the 1953 and 1954 Apache football teams.

A starting tackle on both offense and defense for the 1954 Apache football team (which *Sports Illustrated* named as the top high school team in the nation), Sowash was named All-North Bay League and All-North Coast for his outstanding blocking abilities on offense and his bone – crushing tackles on defense.

Dick Bass (Vallejo Sports Hall of Famer and former great NFL running back) once said "Whether it was in high school, college or the pros, Ed was the best blocker I ever ran behind."

Not only helping the 1953 and 1954 Apache football teams to an 17-0-1 won-loss record and two North Bay League championships, Sowash also played for the Apaches baseball team. An excellent hitter as well as a slick fielding first baseman, Sowash helped the Apaches to a 33-1 won- loss record and two North Bay League championships.

Following his high school graduation in 1955, Sowash enrolled on the campus of the College of the Pacific, where he continued to play football and baseball.

Switching to the tight end position on offense and a linebacker on defense for the Tigers football team, Sowash received All-West Coast honors as a junior.

As a baseball player for the Tigers, Sowash was the team's leading hitter for three years and because of his talents on the baseball diamond he immediately drew attention from many of the pro scouts. Drafted by the Baltimore Orioles in 1959, Sowash played for the Stockton Ports in the Orioles farm system for one year.

Starting his teaching and coaching career in 1960, Sowash coached football for 36 years at the high school level, the junior college level and the major college level, winning numerous league championships, a state championship and a national championship.

Ron Stover

Former Vallejo High School head football coach Bob Patterson called Ron Stover one of the best football players he had ever coached during his 20 plus years of coaching.

Born in Denver, Colorado in 1936, Stover and his family after living in both New Mexico and Oregon would arrive in Vallejo in 1944. Attending McKinley Elementary School and Franklin Jr. High where he played football and baseball, Stover arrived on the campus of Vallejo High School in the fall of 1953 with the idea of concentrating on just playing football.

Playing offensive and defensive end for the 1953 and 1954 Apaches, Stover's play on both sides of the ball ranked him as one of the top players in Northern California. As an offensive end, Stover knew how to get open and once he caught the ball, his balance and size made him extremely tough to bring down. As a defensive end, Stover had the size and strength to stop the run plus the speed and athletic ability to harass the quarterback.

The fifth player in Vallejo High School history to play in the California North/South Shrine All-Star

High School football game in Los Angeles, Stover graduated from high school in 1955 and accepted a scholarship to the University of Oregon, where he became a starter for the Ducks on both offense and defense beginning with the first game of his sophomore year.

A two-time All-American in both his junior and senior year, Stover helped lead the Ducks to the 1957 Pacific Coast Conference Championship and a trip to the 1958 Rose Bowl, where as a junior he would set the Rose Bowl record of 10 receptions for 144 yards against the nations number #1 ranked team, the Ohio State Buckeyes.

As a senior, Stover again received All-American status for his play on the gridiron and would end his college career by playing in both the East-West Shrine All-Star game and the Senior Bowl.

Drafted in 1959 by the Detroit Lions of the NFL and the Toronto Argonauts of the Canadian Football League (CFL), Stover opted to sign with the Argonauts where in 1959 he was named the CFL's Rookie of the Year and All-Pro in 1960 and 1961.

Drafted by the U.S Army in 1962, Stover would rise to the rank of Captain during his three years in the military before heading back to the CFL for the 1965 season. Let go by the Argonauts after the end of the season, the Detroit Lions invited him to play for them in 1966, but Stover decided his playing days were over.

Following his football career, Stover headed back to the Portland, Oregon area where he would work for Willamette Industries (a large lumber and paper company), for 32 years before retiring in 1999 as their Executive Vice-President.

Besides being an All-State player in high school, All-American in college and All-Pro as a professional, Stover was also named as a member of the Oregon Ducks All-Time football team in 1970. Ron Stover was truly a champion at every level of play.

Pete Kalamaras

Pete actually began his sports career as a jockey on thoroughbred races horses. At age twelve and only 104 pounds, he had the size and adventurous spirit to race. Of course, once puberty kicked in, he was no longer small enough to be on the back of a horse. He went on to attend Hogan Junior High where he began his football career. He then went to Vallejo Junior High and Vallejo High School where he excelled as a guard. He was an outstanding player on the 1954 Vallejo High School football team which was featured in *Sports Illustrated* as the top prep team in the nation.

He was named to the All Northern California First Team. He played all conference football at Vallejo Junior College for one year. He then attended the College of the Pacific from 1956-1960. He played football his entire time there. Being only 5'4" and

185 lbs., he was quick which made him a fantastic middle nose guard making great defensive plays. He even was considered by the Dallas Cowboys in 1961; but Pete's real passion was for education.

He received his Doctorate in Education at College of the Pacific. He became a teacher at Juvenile Hall in Fairfield and later the principal. He wrote a teaching program that was adopted by other juvenile halls across the state. Pete enjoyed traveling to Europe, opera and fresh Dungeness crab. He was a great cook, and a devoted father and husband. Many will remember his Olympian spirit. Teammates remember him as one of the toughest, quickest and most competitive players they ever played with.

John Eaton

John Eaton was a star athlete in baseball, basketball and football while growing up in Vallejo in the early 1950's. Not only did he play at the highest level on his local school teams, he also excelled in Legion Baseball, semi-pro baseball and at the collegiate level in football.

Throughout his amazing athletic career, Eaton was given nicknames such as, Johnny "Swisher" Eaton for his team leading basketball statistics and "Mr. TD" for his incredible feats on the gridiron.

Eaton led several of his teams to championship seasons. In baseball, he led his Peanut League baseball team to a 14-0 record and his American Legion Post 104 team to the 1952 District 5 Championship.

In football, Eaton's 1950 Vallejo Jr. High team won the Northern California Junior High School League Title. In 1953, the Vallejo High School Apaches led by Eaton won the North Bay League Championship and in 1954, Eaton led the Vallejo Jr. College Redskins football team to the Golden Valley Conference Championship, in which he was the team captain and star halfback.

Known as a rugged, bruising running back in football, a smooth fielding power hitting shortstop in baseball as well as a team leading scorer as a guard in basketball, Eaton was not afraid of the spotlight as the skill position player in every sport he played, for he always delivered for his teams.

Following graduation from Vallejo Jr. College, Eaton went on to play left halfback for the Sacramento State football team, where it shows his name at the top of many offensive categories for the 1957 Hornets.

Following graduation, Eaton began working as a teacher and coach at Encina High School in Sacramento. It was here Eaton began his football coaching career as well as coaching cross-country, basketball, baseball and gymnastics.

After five years, Eaton left Encina and went to work at Del Campo High School in neighboring Fair Oaks, California, as the Head of the Physical

Education Dept, a position he would hold for the next 37 years.

Retiring from teaching and coaching in 2000, Eaton's record shows coaching football for 41 years. In addition, Eaton served as head coach of the Sacramento Buccaneers semi-pro football team as well as founder and coordinator of the Del Campo Sports-A-Rama.

After all of Eaton's accomplishments in the sports field, Eaton's greatest accomplishment may very well have been his ability to be the consummate team player. Relinquishing the glory of being "Mr. TD" Eaton willingly and happily moved to a blocking back in 1953, his senior year at Vallejo High in order to block for a younger Dick Bass who went on to become one of the greatest athletes in Vallejo history.

One of the most talented and toughest athletes to ever come out of Vallejo, Eaton has always represented Vallejo with dignity and class.

Mark Cameron

Whenever the conversation turns to who were some of the greatest baseball players to come out of Vallejo High School, one name that always seems to be mentioned is that of Mark Cameron.

Born in South Dakota, Cameron at the young age of five would move to Vallejo with his family in 1942 and would attend Curry, Steffan Manor and Highland Elementary Schools before entering Vallejo Jr. High. Playing as much football, basketball and baseball as he could, Cameron would soon develop his skills and by the time he arrived on the campus of Vallejo High in Sept of 1952, it didn't take him long to show the coaches what he could do.

A halfback on the 1953 Apaches football team and a guard on the 1953 basketball team, Cameron's talent and skills helped lead the Apaches to the North Bay League Championship in both sports.

As good as he was in football and basketball, Cameron's favorite sport was baseball. Not only an excellent catcher with an arm that most base runners refused to run against, Cameron was also one of the top hitters on the team as he helped lead the Apaches to two North Bay League Baseball Championships in 1953 and 1954. Batting .321 and .375 for his two seasons with the Apaches, Cameron was named All-North Bay League and along with his teammates Dick Bass and Leon Wilson, was named to the San Francisco Examiner's 1954 Northern California's High School All-Star baseball team.

Graduating in 1954, Cameron entered Vallejo Jr. College and immediately picked up where he had left off in high school, not only leading the Redskins to the 1955 and 1956 Golden Valley Conference Baseball Championship but also quarterbacking the Redskins to the 1955 Golden Valley Conference Football Championship as well.

Named All-Conference in baseball in 1956, Cameron was also named 2nd team All-Northern California because of his talent on the diamond. Following his graduation in 1956, Cameron would take his athletic skills to the campus of Fresno State where he helped the Bulldogs to a 2 nd place finish in the California Collegiate Athletic Association in both the 1957 and 1958 seasons. Besides being named All-Conference as a catcher, Cameron was also named the 1958 MVP for the Bulldogs as he led the team in hitting with a .388 average.

Signing a professional baseball contract with the Fresno Giants in 1960, Cameron would play with them for one year before accepting a teaching position with the Fresno School District. Teaching PE and coaching for four years, Cameron returned to Fresno State to pursue a degree in accounting and after receiving his degree he would become a partner in a large CPA firm.

An active member on numerous civic organization committees, Cameron has also coached youth baseball teams as well as officiating football, basketball and baseball on the high school and college level.

In 1993 Cameron was inducted into the Fresno State Baseball Hall of Fame and the Solano College (Vallejo Jr. College) Sports Hall of Fame in 2005.

Coach Bob Patterson

A four-letter athlete while attending Vallejo High School, Bob Patterson was particularly prominent in football where he played fullback on Coach Kilby's 1925 North Bay League championship team. Upon graduation in 1927, Patterson attended St. Mary's College and quarterbacked the undefeated 1929 championship team. As a senior in 1930, he established a "Little Big Game" record by returning a pass interception for 97 yards to lead his team to victory over Santa Clara.

With his teaching certificate in hand, Coach Patterson returned to Vallejo High in 1934 to coach junior varsity football, basketball, and varsity baseball. After serving in World War II as a naval officer, Coach Patterson returned to Vallejo in 1946 and resumed coaching.

Over the next decade he guided the Vallejo High School Apaches to a number of baseball and football championships. From 1949 to 1956 Coach Patterson's Apache baseball teams won five North Bay League championships and from 1946 to 1956 his Apache football teams won six North Bay League championships including three undefeated seasons: 1949, 1953, and 1954. Coach Patterson's ten year overall North Bay League football conference record was an impressive 78-18-5.

With all his success, Bob always remained humble. When mentioning all of his championships and various awards he would humbly say, "I won this thanks to the kids."

After retiring from coaching in 1956, Coach Patterson served as Athletic Director at Vallejo High School until his retirement.

Coach Dave Thomas

Multi-tasking is a phrase heard often in today's fast paced world. Too bad Dave Thomas invented the method, if not the term, back in the early '20s. Thomas was born in Dudley,Texas, in 1919 and moved to Vallejo with his parents and sister when he was 15 months old. He attended Roosevelt Elementary School and George Washington Junior High School before becoming a member of the first graduating class of Vallejo Junior High School.

He then went on to Vallejo Senior High School. While at VHS, Thomas was elected student body vice president and became a life member of the California Scholastic Federation. Thomas also played on the Class B football team, earning his first letter. He lettered in football, basketball and track, and in 1936 he was a member of Vallejo High's first undefeated football team. He was selected all-league at guard in basketball, eventually graduating from VHS in 1937.

In 1940 he continued his education at Mare Island Apprentice School, graduating in 1942 and becoming a Marine Machinist. Five years later, he transferred to the swing shift and began attending Vallejo Junior College during the day, while working in the evenings. While at Vallejo JC, Thomas played on the basketball team that was ranked among the top 10 teams nationally. He also played football in 1948, being named team captain and also earning the nickname "Gramps," as he was the oldest player in the history of Vallejo Junior College football at the age of 29.

In 1949 he transferred to Chico State University, earning a Bachelor of Arts in Industrial Art Education, and in the summer of 1952 he was accepted to Stanford University's Master's program. In October 1954 he received his Master's degree in Education Administration.

During his years at Chico State, Thomas was offered a job at Vallejo Junior High School. Through the cooperation of the university and the Vallejo school district, he was able to take the job while at the same time complete his college class work. In his first full year of teaching he was appointed assistant football coach with Bob Patterson. This six year assignment produced four championship teams.

Patterson resigned in 1956, and Thomas took over, naming Dick Biama his assistant coach. Together their teams won two league championships in four years. Along with his football duties, Thomas coached track from 1953 to 1winning one league title.

He started coaching the golf team in 1957 and continued to do so for 12 years, winning seven league titles along the way. He was appointed athletic director of Vallejo High School in 1972, and held that position until retiring in 1979.

COACHES BOB PATTERSON AND DAVE THOMAS

16

CONTRIBUTORS

Carol Alaird Weber
Jerry Annoni
Mary Culloty Annoni
Dorothy Bass Atkins
Norman Bass
Walter Blackman
Margaret Cake Neu
Mark Cameron
Mike Campus
Willis (Bill) Clarke
Nancy Osborne Clarke
Sally Case McIver
Bob Coronado
Gent Davis
Leah Bellantini Eaton
John Eaton
Bill Estes
Don Fell
Bernie Fleming
Dale Flowers
Lee Fox
Edie Giant Beck
Barbara Giant Fromm
Cathy Giant Azevedo
Dave Grabest

Dick Hegeman
Yvonne H. Hegeman
D.L. Hurd
Jimmie Jones
Roy Lawson
Steve McLemore
Willis McJunkin
Clark Millholland
Theodore Mitchell
Bill Moore
Linda Nicol Trowbridge
Arlene Passini
Len Read
Don Rodrigo
Bob Sartwell
Joann Simmons Sabilia
Charlie Santiago
Loueen M. Schreiner
Ed Sowash
Doug Stone
Mark Tennis
Maynard Willms
Jimmy Underhill Jr.
Dick Underhill
Adrian Vera

SPECIAL THANKS

Karen de la Peña

Jimmie Jones

Dave Beronio

John F. Kennedy Library - Vallejo

The Greater Vallejo Recreation Department
(Phillip McCoy and Taya De Alba)

&

Waights Taylor Jr.

Apache Blood

A mysterious and ethereal substance
Not really definable nor detectable
For a certainty, we know it exists
Coursing through our very beings
The blood runs deep and true
Nourishing loyalty, respect, pride and love
Forging life long friendships
And more, so much more for each of us
The Apache blood will always be in our hearts
This is why we are a little different
The Apache gift

Dale Flowers

ABOUT THE AUTHORS

Dale Flowers   **Ed Sowash**

Ed Sowash is a retired high school and college football coach. He coached for 36 years—16 in high school, 7 in J.C. and 13 in major college. Born in St. Louis, Missouri, he moved to Vallejo, California, in 1943, so his father could work at Mare Island during WW II. Ed and his wife, Darla live in Windsor, California, in the Sonoma County Wine Country. They have two children, Cindy and Craig, three grand-children, Rachel, Marshall and Karen.

Dale Flowers lives in Aptos, California. He is a retired international organization training and development consultant. He has worked with indigenous peoples and programs in North America, Africa, the Middle East and East Asia. Dale is the father of five sons, six grandchildren and two great grandchildren.